FALLODON PAPERS · *By*

VISCOUNT GREY OF FALLODON K.G.

WOODCUTS BY
ROBERT GIBBINGS

LONDON
CONSTABLE & CO. LTD.

LONDON

PUBLISHED BY

Constable and Company Ltd
10–12 Orange Street W C 2

INDIA

Longmans, Green and Company Ltd
BOMBAY   CALCUTTA   MADRAS

CANADA

Longmans, Green and Company Ltd
TORONTO

First Published .	.	1926
Reprinted (four times) .		1926
Reprinted .	.	1927
Reprinted .	.	1928
Reprinted .	.	1937
Reprinted .	.	1947

Printed in Great Britain by Butler & Tanner Ltd., Frome and London

PREFACE

WITH the exception of the chapter on "Fly-Fishing," which was written to be included here, all the papers in this volume have already appeared in print.

The address on "Recreation" was published separately after it was delivered. I happened to be in the United States not long after the death of Theodore Roosevelt, and it seemed not inappropriate, and was a privilege and pleasure to me, to make a contribution to his memory by giving at his old University an account of an incident in his life in which I had shared.[1]

The other addresses have been printed in the journals or records of the societies or institutions to which they were delivered.

I wish to acknowledge the courtesy of the societies in whose journals severally these papers have appeared.

In ordinary circumstances all these lectures

[1] More than one letter that has been sent me from America assumes that this address on "Recreation" was suggested by some experience or observation of life and habits in the United States. This is not so. What reflections are contained in the address is solely the outcome of experience and life in England.

or addresses would have been first written and
then read from a manuscript. But impaired
sight was unequal to this performance. There
was therefore no original manuscript. Each
address was prepared mentally and delivered
orally like a speech, with the use only of very
slender notes or no notes at all. A verbatim
report was made by a shorthand writer and
revised for the purpose of being printed. But
no amount of revision can quite smooth away
the roughness of expression and arrangement
that is inseparable from oral delivery of an
address that is not read from manuscript and
is too long to be committed to memory.

All the papers were prepared wholly or
mainly at Fallodon, and they contain much
that owes its origin to reflection, observation, or
experience in home or holiday life. " Fallodon
Papers " has, therefore, been chosen as the
most appropriate single title for a varied
collection.

CONTENTS

CONTENTS

I THE PLEASURE OF READING

MY subject, "The Pleasure of Reading," was chosen partly because it is so wide that it covers almost any discursiveness, and partly I have chosen it because I think that modern conditions are putting the pleasure of reading more and more in jeopardy. Some people have such a passion for reading that they will acquire the habit and maintain it against all obstacles. There are others with the inclination and capacity to get that pleasure, but who must find it increasingly difficult under modern conditions to indulge the inclination and cultivate the capacity, and if they do not do so they lose one of the greatest resources and most precious recreations of life. I am using the phrase "The Pleasure of Reading" not in the sense of amusement, but in the sense of that deep and abiding pleasure which increases the more it is indulged. This deserves the name of "recreation," because it actually refreshes and restores as well as entertains. Then there is a third class of people to whom reading, because of the nature of their temperament, will never be any pleasure at all.

These are in no danger whatever from modern conditions. In old days I think it must have been easy to acquire the habit of reading. People stayed for months in the same house without stirring from it even for a night. The opportunities for reading were so many, and the opportunities for doing other things were comparatively so few, that the habit of reading must almost have been forced upon them. I have never been compelled to read " Sir Charles Grandison " myself, but I can well believe that a hundred and fifty years ago there were people who wished " Sir Charles Grandison " even longer than it is.

The first thing necessary to the pleasure of reading is that when people are young they should acquire the habit of reading. This is becoming more and more difficult. Before I was aware of things in the world, the Penny Post had already begun to make a change adverse to reading, by consuming a vast amount of time in correspondence that was unnecessary, trivial, or irksome. Railways have altered people's habits by making them move about much more. But railways have this compensating advantage—that, although they take people much away from home, a long railway journey affords a first-rate opportunity for reading. They were not, therefore, an unmixed disadvantage. But now things are changing. The motor-car is altogether unfavourable to reading. People consume more time in moving about than they did, and they consume it under conditions which, even for people with good eyes, must make reading difficult, if not impossible. The telephone is a deadly disadvantage ; it minces time into fragments and frays the spirit. Wireless, with all its delights, is now being added as a distraction to divert people from time that might be given to the pleasure of reading. The cinematograph is another change in the same direction, and flying is becoming more and more common. All these things must make it more difficult for successive generations to acquire the habit of reading, and, if that habit be acquired, to maintain it. Even before all these changes it was not easy to maintain the habit, but it could be done. There is a story of Auberon Herbert—I do not know whether it is true or not, but I do not mind connecting it with his name, because it is a story I think entirely to his credit, and which I always recall with a sense of satisfaction and encouragement. He was staying in his country home, and some visitors were announced. He received them with perfect good manners, and, after a cordial welcome, he said to them, " And now what would you like to do ?—we are reading." We need more and more of that spirit.

A further disadvantage to reading is the great development of picture papers. Picture papers are tending to divert people not only from reading, but from thought. Where one

used to see people get into a railway carriage
and settle down to a book, they now come with
an armful of picture papers and look at the
pictures with more or less transient amusement,
one after the other, and so pass the time. I
found the other day a person who during the
war between the Turks and the Greeks expressed
an opinion rather in favour of the Turks,
because he or she (I will not reveal even the
sex) said that, judging by the pictures in the
papers, Mustapha Kemal looked rather a good
sort of fellow.

In connection with this danger to reading
I would like to quote to you what I consider
a notable sonnet of Wordsworth, remarkable
for the fact that it was written in 1846, when
he was seventy-six years old, and that yet
contains a good deal of his young fire, remarkable in that it was written when illustrated
papers must have been in their infancy, and
remarkable for the prescience with which he
foresaw the danger to reading from the development of illustration, which was then so very
little advanced. This is the sonnet :

> Discourse was deemed Man's noblest attribute,
> And written words the glory of his hand :
> Then followed Printing with enlarged command
> For thought—dominion vast and absolute
> For spreading truth, and making love expand.
> Now Prose and verse sunk into disrepute
> Must lacquey a dumb Art that best can suit
> The taste of this once-intellectual Land.
> A backward movement surely have we here,
> From manhood—back to childhood ; for the age—

Back towards caverned life's first rude career.
Avaunt this vile abuse of pictured page !
Must eyes be all in all, the tongue and ear
Nothing ? Heaven keep us from a lower stage.

There is a good deal of power in that sonnet, but the remarkable thing is its prescience. If these recent developments are endangering the pleasure of reading, as undoubtedly they are, by making it more and more difficult to acquire the habit, let me suggest one thing which may be a help to maintain it. It is this : Plan reading beforehand ; have always in mind three or four books which you have decided you wish to read ; have the books at hand so that when the opportunity comes for reading the choice may be readily made ; otherwise, you may be staying in a country house, and something, not reading, may have been planned for the afternoon ; stormy weather causes that plan to be cancelled, and two or three hours are thrown into your lap—a little tumble-in of time—an unlooked-for opportunity for reading. We may, any of us, with such an opportunity find ourselves in the middle of a good library, and yet, if we have not already thought to ourselves and determined on some book which we wish to read, when the opportunity comes the greater part of the time may be lost in the difficulty of making a choice. I offer this as a practical counsel, and it is easy to apply it. *The Times Literary Supplement* and any number of literary reviews are constantly recalling old books to mind, or suggesting new ones

which we think we should like to read, and
with this help it is very easy to have a plan
ready which will secure that no opportunity
for reading is lost when it occurs.

Now I pass on to consider one or two aspects
of the actual pleasure of reading. Poetry, of
course, comes first and highest. I am not going
to talk about the pleasure in pure poetry,
because to all who have it, it is so well known
that no words of mine will increase the pleasure.
To those who have not got it, no words that I
could utter would give it. I refer to the
abiding pleasure that people who love poetry
get from rhythm, the music of words, and
imagery. As an illustration of what I mean
I would give Keats's three odes, "To a
Nightingale," "To a Grecian Urn," and "To
Autumn," or the irresistible charm of the
simplest songs of Shakespeare—such as "Fear
no more the heat of the sun." Those I give as
an instance of pleasure in pure poetry. Not
everybody is open to it. Some one, and some
one of considerable intelligence and intellectual
attainment, once said to me that the only effect
produced by poetry was the reflection how
much better the thing could be expressed in
prose. Imagine taking Keats's "Ode to
Autumn" and expressing it better in prose!
But besides this there are further pleasures in
poetry of a deeper kind, but less obvious.
There is the poetry which presents to us great
thought in words and in forms that not only
stir the intellect, but rouse emotion. I will say

nothing in that connection of Shakespeare, because I am going to take a smaller illustration. I do not talk about Shakespeare for fear of falling into platitude. When I went out of office after eleven years of it, very tired, and for the time not fit for anything, I spent some weeks alone in the country. During that time I read, or re-read, several of Shakespeare's plays. The impression produced upon me by his incredible power and range was really that of awe ; I felt almost afraid to be alone in the room with him—as if I were in the presence of something supernatural. Therefore, if I do not draw illustrations from Shakespeare, it is not from want of appreciation of his stature and genius. The instance I would take is of poetry that deals with great thought, doing for us what is essential if our pleasure is to be really permanent, making our minds open on the infinite, making us think thoughts which we know are too great for any words to express, and bringing something, that before was beyond our comprehension, within the grasp of it. I will take an instance from another poet. I will ask you to think of Browning. In some passages it seems to me Browning is eminently successful in this power of bringing something of the infinite within our reach. He is not always successful. There are some passages in which, after we have disentangled laboriously the mass of words in order to discover the great thought which has been captured in them, we find that the great thought has

escaped, or at any rate that we cannot find it.
A simile is suggested to me by Browning's own
words, " Fancies that broke through language
and escaped." Any one who is familiar with
Browning's poems, such as " Rabbi Ben Ezra,"
" Abt Vogler," " Bishop Blougram's Apology,"
and " Paracelsus," will know what I mean
when I say that Browning adds to the pleasure
of poetry by bringing those who read him into
contact with great thoughts.

The comment I would make on Tennyson is
exactly the reverse. I do not mean by the
" reverse " that Tennyson's thought is small
and that of Browning great. Tennyson deals
with great thought, too, but by his extraordinary mastery of the music of words and his
wonderful lucidity of expression he sometimes
makes the thought seem not so great as it
really is. At times he makes something of the
infinite almost finite. This comment on Tennyson is not intended to be either criticism or
praise. But it is worth bearing in mind that,
when Tennyson seems very simple, the thought
may be great, and that the difference between
Tennyson and Browning is not in the greatness
of the thought, but in the different ways in
which the two men treat it. Take, for instance, the eleven opening stanzas of " In
Memoriam " ; they are very simple to read
—so simple that perhaps we may read them
without realizing how great the thought is.
Browning treats of the same kind of thought,
and when he does so we have no doubt that it

is great. Sometimes he makes it even obscure, whereas Tennyson makes it so simple that he deceives us as to its depth, as a very limpid and clear water will seem more shallow than it really is. So much I would say about that part of the pleasure of great poetry. Beyond the music of words, the rhythm, the imagery, there is the great thought which touches us with emotion.

But there is more than this pleasure to be found in poetry. I once stayed in a house as a guest for a night where a formidable volume was kept. It was a volume of which every page had a series of set questions designed to draw out the opinions of those to whom the volume was presented. I was, happily, too young and too insignificant to be asked to go through that ordeal, but I was shown the volume, and one of the guests who had preceded me had been John Morley. He had not been spared the ordeal, and he had gone through it in all seriousness, and opposite the deadly question, " Who is your favourite poet ? " he had written the name of " Wordsworth." I, too, should have written the name of Wordsworth—certainly I should write it now. It is worth considering why John Morley wrote " Wordsworth," and why many of us would name Wordsworth as our favourite poet. Of course, it is impossible to account satisfactorily for this, to catch one's own thought and feeling so clearly as to justify this preference. But one reason, no doubt, is that for endur-

ing satisfaction in poetry we want strength.
Browning has splendid strength which never
fails or falters ; but Wordsworth, too, is
strong. If he expresses, as he sometimes does,
great dejection, great depression, he never
rests or brings his poem to an end till he stands
with both feet planted on firm ground by some
thought which has pulled him up, rescued him
from depression, and made him erect and
confident. It is interesting to compare Wordsworth and Shelley in this respect. It does not
add to the pleasure of reading to exalt one
author at the expense of another, and I am
not introducing this comparison for the purpose
of depreciating Shelley, but you will notice
that Shelley is sometimes content to leave you
with a cry of despair. Wordsworth, after
expressing deep dejection, never ends till he has
become confident and strong again. You will
find instances of what I mean in Wordsworth's
" Lines on the Death of Fox " ; you will find
it in " The Leech Gatherer," and you will find
it in the " Afterthought " (of the Duddon
sonnets), and in many other places. There is
a further pleasure in poetry which is that of
intimacy. When people say Wordsworth is the
poet they read most, or the poet they like best,
what they really feel is that they have a certain
intimacy with Wordsworth—that Wordsworth
has revealed to them some of their own experience, expressed something of which they were
barely conscious, and revealed to them other
things which were really in them, but of which

they were unconscious. In this way there has come a feeling which can best be described as that of intimacy, which, apart altogether from his merits as a poet, makes Wordsworth peculiarly attractive to the reader. Having said so much about him, I would only add this—that when you are quite confident that you appreciate Wordsworth's poetry, that you set it high, that you are grateful for it, even that you have some reverence for it, you are entitled to get a certain amusement out of his foibles. One form of amusement is easily found by reading the extraordinarily stiff or trivial labels which he chose to attach as titles to some of his poems. " Ode to Duty " is not a title which attracted me very much. The poem attracts and holds me ; but the title did not draw me to the poem. " Resolution and Independence " does not suggest poetry at all. Happily in this instance Wordsworth vouchsafes an alternative title, " The Leech Gatherer." " Lines on Hearing that the Dissolution of Mr. Fox was Hourly Expected," " Extempore Effusion on the Death of James Hogg "— neither of these titles prepares you for the beautiful things which these poems contain. Then we get " Incident in the Life of a Favourite Dog," followed by " Tribute to the Memory of the same Dog," and, finally, " On Seeing a Needle-Case in the Form of a Harp." I have laughed often over these titles, and it is right that any one who is quite sure of his admiration for Wordsworth and his gratitude

to him should indulge in this amusement ; but
to people who do not appreciate Wordsworth's
poetry, and who laugh at these things, I would
say, be sure that your laughter is not of that
kind which has been compared to the " crack-
ling of thorns under a pot."

I would say this further : the habit of
reading poetry should be acquired when people
are young.   What we acquire and learn to love
when we are young stands by us through life.
It has been difficult in all ages for people who
are past middle life to appreciate the genius of
new poets who have arisen in their lifetime.
Wordsworth wrote his best poetry long before
Queen Victoria was born.   Shelley and Keats
were dead before she came to the throne, but
they came by their own in public estimation
in the Victorian age, and, having come by their
own, they have little difficulty in maintaining
it as the generations go on.   It is astonishing
to look back and see how people of real literary
ability and power have been absolutely blind
to the merits of poetry written when they
themselves were in middle life, which we, who
have come after them, recognize at once as
being of the first rank.   Let us make sure of the
poetry that we like while we are young ; then
we keep it easily through life, for it is difficult
to be certain of appreciating and enjoying new
poetry after we have passed middle age.

Next to poetry I put novels—the great
novels of character. They must be long to
be great. It needs a long book to present a

character so that it can be really grasped and understood. Short stories, however vivid their presentation of character, are something like a brilliant pen-and-ink sketch. The great novel, on the other hand, makes the characters stand out as if they were sculptured. Of such great novels it is worth noting that some of the most famous depend not entirely, but to some extent, upon dealing with love as passion ; by this the interest is heightened and their enduring place in literature is secured. The first half of *Pamela*, for instance, *Jane Eyre*, *Anna Karénine*, are all highly sexed novels, and much of their interest depends upon this. After reading a novel of this kind, one is apt to feel that no great novel can be written unless it does introduce this element of passion. If any one thinks this, it is worth his while reading first *Jane Eyre*, and then Jane Austen's *Emma*—the one as devoid of passion as the other is conspicuous for it. Thackeray's novels are great without passion. So you realize that there is no law to the great novelists, and that, while some of the greatest of them seem to have thought it necessary to deal with that vast problem in human nature in their books, there are others who have made little use of it, and who yet—as Jane Austen and Thackeray have done—achieve their prominent places as securely as the others. Jane Austen is to me the greatest wonder amongst novel writers. I do not mean that she is the greatest novel writer, but she seems to me the greatest

wonder. Imagine, if you were to instruct an
author or an authoress to write a novel under
the limitations within which Jane Austen
writes ! Supposing you were to say, " Now,
you must write a novel, but you must have no
heroes or heroines in the accepted sense of the
word. You may have naval officers, but they
must always be on leave or on land, never
on active service. You must have no striking
villains ; you may have a mild rake, but keep
him well in the background, and if you are
really going to produce something detestable,
it must be so because of its small meannesses,
as, for instance, the detestable Aunt Norris in
Mansfield Park ; you must have no very exciting plot ; you must have no thrilling adven-
tures ; a sprained ankle on a country walk
is allowable, but you must not go much
beyond this. You must have no moving
descriptions of scenery ; you must work without the help of all these ; and as to passion,
there must be none of it. You may, of course,
have love, but it must be so carefully handled
that very often it seems to get little above the
temperature of liking. With all those limitations you are to write, not only one novel, but
several, which, not merely by popular appreciation, but by the common consent of the
greatest critics, the greatest literary minds of
the generations which succeed you, shall be
classed among the first rank of the novels
written in your language in your country."
Of course, it is possible to say that Jane Austen

achieves this, though her materials are so slight because her art is so great. Perhaps, however, so long as the materials are those of human nature, they are not slight.

Another class of novel depending not so much for interest upon development of character is that of adventure, novels of the Homeric kind, such as those of Dumas, for instance— *Monte Cristo* and the whole series of *The Three Musketeers*. They give a pleasure of a different kind from the pleasure we take in the novels of character, but it is a kind by no means to be overlooked or neglected, and it may be a very great pleasure. There is a story told—I forget where I came across it, and I have never been able to verify it—of a man of the world in middle life, not liable to youthful enthusiasms, who one evening fell to reading *Monte Cristo*. His wife retired to bed at the usual time. He sat up reading, and in the small hours of the night he suddenly burst into his wife's room, who knew nothing at all about the book, and informed her in a transport of enthusiasm that Dantès had escaped from the Château d'If. The pleasure these novels of adventure give is one to be cultivated ; they are a great class of novels.

Then there is a third category that suggests itself to me—the novels which depend on their humour for their permanency and the delight which they give. *Pickwick*, of course, is an instance. On this I would observe that the quality of humour and wit—though all of it

which is brilliant of every kind may excite our
admiration or give us pleasure at the moment
—must, if it is to be enduring, be humour
which is innocent and clean. I would like to
suggest to you an example. I think it comes to
this : any pleasure to be lasting, so that we
wish to return to it and to think of it again
and again, must have its hold, not only upon
the intellect, but upon the affections. There is
a great deal of humour and wit which appeals
only to the intellect, but gets no hold on the
affections. It has its brilliant success with us
when we first meet it, but it does not abide
with us and increase our pleasure as we
go on in years. Let us compare *Tristram
Shandy* with *The Sentimental Journey*. The same
exquisite art is in both. *The Sentimental
Journey* I have read with great entertainment
more than once, but it is not lovable as is
Tristram Shandy. *Tristram Shandy* always keeps
its fresh hold upon our affections. Why is
this ? There are conversations and situations
in *Tristram Shandy* which live and endure, and
are a perpetual delight to succeeding generations because of the endearing innocence and
simplicity with which Uncle Toby is intruded
into them. Uncle Toby is the antiseptic
which has kept, and always will keep, *Tristram
Shandy* a fresher book than *The Sentimental
Journey*.

I will only mention one or two other classes
of books. There are the great histories and the
great biographies. From the point of view of

pleasure I would observe—and this I borrow from some past number of *The Times Literary Supplement*—that it is the biographies of literary men which are the most interesting. Next come the biographies of great soldiers, which are interesting from the point of view of the art of war. The dullest biographies of all are those of politicians. This is because the biography of a politician is apt to develop into an account of the politics in which he was concerned. The literary man, on the other hand, is not often concerned in public events, and those characters and aspects of his life which are selected for his biography are remarkable in the perspective, not only of his generation, but also in that of generations that come after. Think of the biographies most frequently quoted—Boswell's *Life of Johnson* pre-eminently ; Lockhart's *Scott* ; Moore's *Life of Byron* ; all biographies of literary men.

Finally, I would say a word about books on Nature. It was suggested to me by this : When I was about two-and-twenty I read Kingsley's *Prose Idylls*, *Chalk Stream Studies*, *A Charm of Birds*, *My Winter Garden*, and others. At that time in my life I should have put them in the very first rank of books about Nature. I preferred them at that time above White's *Selborne* or Izaak Walton's *Compleat Angler*. As years went on, I found the pleasure in White's *Selborne* and Walton's *Angler* increase more and more, and after some thirty years or so I read the *Prose Idylls* again, and I found that they had lost their charm for me. I am somewhat puzzled myself to know why, but I think I do know. This is worth while considering. It is not merely that Izaak Walton and Gilbert White had greater art in literature than Charles Kingsley. Charles Kingsley was no mean writer; he knew how to write, he could write well. The real difference is that Kingsley, when writing about Nature, has not the quality of repose, that atmosphere of calm and contemplation, which is found in writers like Izaak Walton and Gilbert White. If books about Nature are to live, they must not be descriptions written at the moment of rapture; they must be books written as the result of observation, which recall and convey the emotion after it has sunk into the mind. Wordsworth said that poetry was emotion recollected in tranquillity. I will not discuss how far this is true of poetry, but I think it is true for books on Nature. These should be the result of long observation, much feeling, and tranquillity, and then the effect upon the reader is one of calm and contemplation, and brings that sense of leisure and repose for which, in these days, we are more and more grateful. The works of W. H. Hudson have this quality.

I will conclude with one or two general remarks on the pleasure of reading. Let us not neglect as we grow older the pleasure of re-reading books which we remember we liked when we were young, but which we have greatly forgotten and which we should like to read again. Some, as we have seen, will have lost their charm, but others we shall find more interesting than before. For instance, I read *Middlemarch* after an interval of about thirty years, because I remembered having liked it. The conclusion on re-reading it was that it must have been impossible in youth to have appreciated half its merit. I certainly got pleasure from reading it when I was young, but I got more pleasure on reading it again years afterward.

The great books have stood the test of time because they possess in an unusual degree the power of satisfying human needs, and giving sustained human pleasure ; and it is a great mistake to let new literature divert us from reading the old. Isaac Disraeli says somewhere that great books lead us to a proper perspective and sense of the values of life. The sentence is something to this effect : " He who is not familiarized with the finest passages of the finest writers will one day be mortified to observe that his best thoughts are their indifferent ones."

This last word I would say on the pleasure of reading : It was Tennyson who said, " I like these large still books." It is the large still books that give the most abiding pleasure, but, if we are to read them and appreciate them, we must sometimes be still ourselves ; we must reach that calm and contemplative mood which makes us receptive of the best things in literature. Bacon, in his *Essay on*

Study, says, " Study is for delight, for ornament, and for ability. For delight its chief use is in privateness and retirement " ; and Walton, at the end of his most famous and beautiful book, puts simply this quotation :

Study to be quiet.

II PLEASURE IN NATURE

THE subject on which I have under-
taken to say something is important
for all persons who are concerned about
education, yet it is a somewhat difficult one to
approach from the point of view of teaching.
The subject I have taken is that of " Pleasure in
Outdoor Nature." Now, given that a teacher
is capable and a pupil is willing, you can
make sure of teaching knowledge. You can
impart knowledge, but you cannot make sure
of imparting pleasure. In order to illustrate
what I mean I will mention the game of golf.
Anybody can be taught the rules of the game
of golf and how to play golf. One person may
turn out to be a very good player and another
an indifferent·player, yet even an indifferent
player may find so much pleasure in the game
that it becomes an enthusiasm and a passion.
But in the case of another person with equal
aptitude for the game, though you can make
certain of teaching him the rules and how to
play, you may find that, instead of imparting
pleasure, the more he knows the more bored he
gets, and he leaves it off. Thus you can make

a certainty of imparting knowledge, but pleasure you cannot impart, unless there is in the
person taught some natural aptitude and
capacity for enjoyment. Nevertheless, the imparting of pleasure, it seems to me, is a very
important part of education. There is a great
deal of discontent in the world ; some is due
to poverty, to ill-health, to want of leisure, to
overwork, to unhappy outward circumstances ;
moralists would say that much of it is due to
the fact that people have not sufficient moral
basis, to which an American girl is said to have
retorted, " No doubt people who are good are
happy, but they do not have a good time."
That sort of discontent with which the moralist
or economist has to deal is outside my subject.
The proposition I would put to you is this,
that people, who have a reasonable amount of
leisure, should have a habit of spending that
leisure and a capacity for spending it in a way
that brings interest and pleasure, and that
this is a great factor in making life contented.
That is the proposition. For this purpose, if
you can impart the power of taking real pleasure in the best poetry and the best literature,
no doubt you will have given the most easily
accessible and most permanent and lasting
form of making leisure satisfactory ; because
books, even the best, are easily accessible, and
all that is necessary for the enjoyment of them
is that you should, in fine weather, find some
quiet spot out of doors, or that you should have
access to a room in which there is no telephone.

Books I would put first. By books I mean
the power of taking pleasure in the best
literature. But next to books I would put the
capacity for finding pleasure in Outdoor
Nature. There are two great advantages in it ;
two great qualities that belong to it. One is
that it means a capacity for taking pleasure in
common things. The beauty of the world
and the interesting things in wild Nature are
there for everybody to enjoy, and the fact that
one person enjoys them does not diminish the
power of others to enjoy them provided only
that everybody, who takes pleasure in Outdoor
Nature, will observe the one simple rule, which
is far too often broken, that you should take
your pleasure in Outdoor Nature without
destroying or disturbing. As long as you do
that, your pleasure is not diminishing any one
else's pleasure. For instance, supposing you
are in one of the London parks, and there
happens to be, as happily there often is, a
thrush or blackbird singing, and you stop to
enjoy the song, the fact that some one else
stops to enjoy it does not diminish your
pleasure, it increases it ; but if some one
throws a stone at the bird, he destroys your
pleasure.

The other quality is that the best kind of
pleasure in Outdoor Nature does not depend
on novelty, but upon enjoying things which
recur in the seasons of the year. Every season
of the year brings its own aspects of beauty or
its own subjects of interest. They recur year

after year ; it is precisely because of this that
they become increasingly familiar, and we look
forward to them every year. If you wish to
cultivate pleasure, there are three parts of it
to be cultivated. One is anticipation, another
realization, and the third is retrospect. You
can only have perfect anticipation of pleasure
if it is a pleasure you have enjoyed before, so
that you know before it arrives exactly what
it is like and the sort of feeling you are going
to get. Outdoor Nature has a succession of
seasons and every year they bring round the
same procession of beauty and interest. I
am going to illustrate these general proposi-
tions from the study of birds, but please
do not think I am going to give instruction
to you about birds. My own knowledge
is not that of an expert. Like many people
who have been at the mercy of public life,
which is a very tyrannous affair, I have
passed the age of sixty and still have such
deficiency of information that I am not
really capable of giving instruction about
anything.

What I would like to try to convey to you,
having had much pleasure myself in the
observation of birds, is that you can get
pleasure from observing them. The word
" consider " is used in the Bible in just the
sense that applies to watching objects in
Nature ; the sense of giving attention in order
to appreciate and admire. " Hast thou considered my servant Job ? " " Consider the lilies

of the field." I want this afternoon to *consider* certain birds and certain aspects of them in order that we may understand, appreciate, and admire them. Of course there are some people who take no pleasure in birds ; they have not the capacity for doing so. But it is known to everybody that to a large number of people birds are a source of very great interest and pleasure. Why is this so ? Because they have certain remarkable and attractive natural qualities. First of all, there is the power of flight, in itself a thing worth considering. The flight of different species of birds, the manner of their flying, differs so that an expert can tell by the manner of a bird's flight what species of bird it is. There are, amongst our common birds, all sorts and manners and ways of flying, from the buoyant and prolonged flight of the common gulls down to the rising and falling flight of the woodpeckers, which seems to be so precarious that you doubt sometimes whether the woodpecker will be able to fly to the next tree. On the other hand, if you will lie on your back on a fine day, you may see gulls sailing high in the air, without apparent effort or movement of wing, as though it was not necessary for them to descend at all ; and between these two, the apparently inexhaustible power of the gull to sustain itself in the air, and the rising and falling flight of the woodpecker whose wings are weak— between these there are all sorts and degrees of the power of flight, and from that point

of view alone our common birds become of
interest.

The next aspect of birds is their plumage and
wonderful variety of colouring which presents
all sorts of questions to which I can give you
no answer. Why should males, for instance,
have a bright colour and females a comparatively dull colour, as in the case of the chaffinch
and bullfinch ; while in other cases, for instance, the hedge sparrow (which I prefer to
call the dunnock because it has nothing to do
with the sparrow), both the males and females
are of the same colour ? And then you have a
further variety of plumage when you come to
the common wild duck, of which the drake is
for the greater part of the year a very brilliant
bird with most beautiful colours and the female
is sober-coloured. But when the female is
nesting the male bird, the drake, undergoes a
change ; he loses all that bright colour and
becomes a shabby and dowdy object, and, as if
ashamed of himself, slinks out of sight, so that,
when the duck comes on the water with her
brood of young ducklings, the drake has
disappeared. There are other waterfowl, especially some foreign ones, some of them very
nearly related to our own common wild duck,
which have an entirely different plan as regards
plumage. In some the male is brilliant, but the
female is also brilliant, and where that is the
case the male bird is allowed to retain the
brilliancy of his colour all the year round.
In other cases the male bird is sober-coloured

like the female and he retains the same colour
all the year round. And there is this curious
accompaniment of this variety of habit, so far
as I have been able to observe, where the drake
remains the same colour as the female throughout the year, whether brilliant or sober-
coloured ; when the female has hatched her
brood of young ducklings, the drake helps to
tend and bring them up, whereas our own wild
drake and other drakes, which are brilliant at
one time, but dull at another, do not go with
the young brood at all to help to bring them
up. Why this is so I cannot say, but it is a
matter of interest to find in some species of
birds males brilliant and females sober-coloured,
in other species both sexes sober-coloured, in
others both sexes brilliant-coloured, as, for
instance, the kingfisher, and in some species
the male brilliant-coloured for only one part
of the year and sober-coloured for the other
part. The reasons for all these different
arrangements in the plumage of different
species are subjects of speculation.

The third aspect of birds I would take is the
fact that they lay eggs of such various colours
and build nests of such various shapes and
substance. If I had to give a prize for nest-
building amongst our common birds I would
give it to the long-tailed tit, which is a bird
distributed over the whole of Great Britain.
You meet with it frequently, from Sutherland
to the South of England, in every county
where I have been and where there is anything

like a reasonable amount of plantation. It
builds a most elaborate nest, and the whole
time taken for the building of the nest, the
hatching of the eggs, and the fledging of
the young is a very long one—much longer
than in the case of any other British bird I
know.

When I was in office I had a cottage in the
country to which I went at week-ends, and
one Sunday morning before the middle of
March I observed from the window a pair of
long-tailed tits building their nest in a sweet-
briar hedge. When I went out and looked at
the nest it was then like an ordinary nest, cup-
shaped. A long-tailed tit is not content with
that, but it builds a nest like a bag with a hole
near the top. Every week I went down there
the building and business of the nest was
going on. It so happened that the 19th of May
that year was a Sunday and I was at my
cottage. It also happened that this particular
day, about noon, was the time when the young
birds first came out of the nest. It also happened that I was standing close by the nest at
the time when the little birds first came out
of it. Thus you will see that this pair of long-
tailed tits required about two months and a
half from the time they began to build their
nest to the time the young came out of it.
During all those weeks, when I could be there,
the nest was a subject of interest to me,
and many of you living in the country may
have the same experience provided that you

will yourselves, and are able to induce other people to observe the rule, not to disturb or destroy.

Long-tailed tits are particularly interesting from another point of view. The birds go in a company and the brood remains together all the autumn and winter, but early in March you will see the long-tailed tits in pairs, and if you will look closely you will see about that time that they have some little nesting material in their beaks, and if you watch them you will see them going to the nest and you can locate it. Sometimes it is rather high up in the fork of a tree, generally oak or ash, but as often as not it is only four or five feet from the ground in a gorse bush or an ordinary hedge. Whether they think they are so small that you do not see them or whether they are so intensely busy in their work, it so happens that they are not at all shy, and you can stand at a distance of three yards from the nest quite openly and watch them build. You will see first one bird and then the other get into the nest when it is in cup shape and make it round and smooth by rubbing its breast round and round against the wall of the nest. You will see it arch its head over the sides of the nest and pull some of the outside over and inwards, weaving it thus ; and when the nest is completed outside, the birds will line the inside with feathers. Then if you like you can help in the building of the nest. If you can collect small feathers and put them close to the nest, you can stand near

and see the long-tailed tits take the feathers
that you put for them and use them in their
nest-building. When the young birds have
fledged you can, without doing any harm, take
the nest and examine it, because I have never
known long-tailed tits use their nest a second
time. I have been told that the feathers used
in the lining of a long-tailed tit's nest have
been counted to number more than nine
hundred. That seems incredible ; I have not
verified it, but any of you can do so.

It does not do to take every nest after the
birds are fledged, because some of them are
used again. I have known a blackbird rear
two successive broods in the same season in the
same nest, and after that a pair of pied wagtails
took the nest, made a new cup in it, and reared
their young in it.

Next let us take an instance of a bird which
builds not only one nest, but more than one.
The common wren often builds more nests
than are used for eggs. The nest that is used
for eggs is lined with feathers, but one or more
nests are often built apparently with equal
skill, except that they are not lined with
feathers, and have no eggs put into them.
These nests are often referred to as " unoccu-
pied dwellings," but it is not an accurate
description. I found one of these nests near
my house one summer, and in the autumn and
winter I used occasionally to go after sunset
and look at the nest, and whenever I went a
single wren came out of it. So it was quite

clear that that particular nest, though not built for eggs, was used by a wren as a bedroom through the autumn and winter, though I cannot be sure whether it was the same wren that built the nest.

Next I come to a less cheerful subject in the way of nests. If you study the habits of birds, you will find at one end of the scale what I would call the creditable and at the other end the discreditable aspect of a habit, and at the discreditable end you will generally find the cuckoo. Please do not think that I do not like cuckoos. I am very fond of them, but I can only defend my liking for cuckoos in the way that I have heard some people defend their liking for a somewhat disagreeable friend. They usually say, " I cannot help liking him, I know him so well." As you know, the cuckoo has no nest of its own. It uses other birds' nests ; it does not sit on its own eggs, and the young cuckoo turns the other birds out of the nest. Some thirty years ago, when I was in office, I found at one week-end a dunnock's nest with a cuckoo's egg among those that the dunnock had laid. Close by I found a whitethroat's nest with eggs. I came down at the end of the following week and visited both nests to see how they were getting on. In the dunnock's nest there was lying there at the bottom, a young cuckoo, alone, naked, blind, hideous, and apparently helpless. I then went to look at the whitethroat's nest, and found that there were recently hatched

young birds in number corresponding with the
eggs I had seen there a week before. I bor-
rowed, temporarily, one of the little birds from
that nest and put it in the dunnock's nest with
the little cuckoo, and saw that apparently
helpless hideous thing turn the little whitethroat
out of the nest. You can try this for yourselves ; and if you cannot find a newly hatched
bird to put in with the cuckoo, you can induce
the cuckoo to perform by making a small piece
of wool into a ball, very lightly and loosely
made, about the size of a recently hatched
little bird. You can now see the cuckoo's
methods of procedure exhibited on a film, and
the experiment I have mentioned can be made
by anybody who can find a young cuckoo in a
nest : then you can watch it repeat the performance for yourselves ; you can do this,
provided you use a certain amount of tact
and care, without disturbing either nest, and
without injury to any of the objects on which
you are experimenting.

A further aspect of birds, perhaps the most
attractive of all, is the gift that some of them
have of song. If people wish to appreciate our
common birds, they must learn their songs.
There is more pleasure to those who know them
in the songs of birds than in almost any other
aspect of bird life. It takes some trouble to
learn the songs, but it is almost essential to
pleasure in bird life to have a reasonably good
knowledge of bird songs. The best time to get
this knowledge is from the middle of April to

the middle of May, when all the birds are in full song, when the summer birds are here or are on the way to us, and the leaves are not fully open on all the trees, so that you get the best view of the birds. The songs of our common birds are no doubt known to many of you, and I would only say one or two things about them. First of all, if you are fond of songs of birds, make a point of not letting any single month of the year go by without hearing the robins and the wrens sing, because these two birds can be heard every month in the year. If there is a very cold and severe month, you may not be able to hear them, but in any average year you can hear them sing in every month. And the wren's song is remarkable for its exceeding loudness compared with the size of the bird. You will not have much difficulty in getting close to the wren, when it is singing, and if you consider the smallness of its body, the loudness of its song, the vehemence of it, and the animation of the body, well, really, I have sometimes been afraid that the little body would burst and be shattered by the vehemence of the song. These two birds you can hear sing in every month of the year, but there are other birds that sing only for a few months.

The blackbird is one of our best singers, but you will not, as a rule, hear much of its song before March or after the month of June. I have known of people hearing blackbirds in the month of January, but when I have been able to investigate the matter, I have found a missel

thrush to be the bird they had heard singing.
In the early part of the year the hearing of the
first blackbird's song is a thing specially to
look forward to, precisely because you have not
heard it for so long. This is an instance where
anticipation increases pleasure. And then, as
the season goes on, there come the summer
birds which have spent the winter in North
Africa or even farther south. There is not only
pleasure in hearing their songs each spring for
the first time, but there is something romantic
in thinking of the immenseness of the journey
they may have accomplished since you heard
them the year before. A swallow, ringed in
this country in the summer, has, I am told,
been found as far south as Natal, thousands of
miles away, yet, if all went well, that swallow
would have returned to this country, and to
the particular spot in this country, where it had
been reared. And so with other birds.

The anticipation in the spring of the coming
of these birds from the places where they have
spent the winter, is a thing to which one looks
forward with the greatest interest. You will
probably hear the first blackcap, the first
willow warbler, and the first wood warbler, and
so forth each year in much the same place as
you heard it before, and so, when one gets fond
of these birds and gets the habit of listening for
them in the same place at the same time every
spring, the satisfaction of having your anticipation realized, of hearing the same song in the
same place for perhaps thirty years, and know-

ing that same bird or its successor has come back to the same spot, is a satisfaction which gives us peculiar pleasure.

It is not only of the birds which come to us in the summer that I would say something. There is also the other migration to look forward to, the birds which come to us from farther north or farther east to spend the winter in this country. One familiar instance is the woodcock. Many woodcocks breed in this country, and presumably never leave these islands. But the great majority of the woodcocks we have in the autumn and winter come from farther north or farther east. They cross the North Sea. The North Sea is a formidable width for small birds to cross. We are told by those who have studied these things that there was a time when the North Sea was all land, and perhaps that is the reason why some birds undertake this tremendous journey across the North Sea. If the species came that way when the North Sea did not exist, I suppose they may have kept up the habit when the North Sea was gradually formed, though I am not sure whether birds existed at the time when there was no North Sea.

I was once lying on the sand hills by the shore in Northumberland on a fine, bright, still day about the end of November. I was lying on my back looking up at the sky and I saw a woodcock arrive evidently from a great height with great velocity behind its descent. It slanted down over me at tremendous speed.

It descended with wings rigid, not quite fully
expanded ; it seemed to come with precipitate
and great speed from very high up. It lit in
the rough grass about seventy yards behind
me. I wished to know if it was tired after its
long flight, so I went to see how it was. It rose
several yards in front of me and flew away
over the fields inland with no sign of being
tired, and from that I judged that in the
ordinary way, with fine weather, birds can
cross the North Sea quite easily without being
exhausted or tired. When they meet with
bad weather they arrive very exhausted and
no doubt many perish on the way.

However, it is not very surprising that the
woodcock crosses the North Sea, when the
smallest bird we have, the golden-crested wren,
crosses it in numbers every autumn. The
golden-crested wren is very common in this
country wherever there is woodland, especially
fir trees. If you get to know their song you
can realize how common they are. Many of
them breed in this country and probably never
leave it. They are not very shy ; you can get
close to them, and the only difficulty in watching them is that they are so very restless. Now
the next time you have the opportunity of
getting close to one, just consider the fact that,
though that particular bird may never have
crossed the North Sea, thousands and thousands of golden-crested wrens exactly like it,
as small and apparently as weak, do cross
the North Sea every year. One observer in

Heligoland years ago, in 1882, saw such a mass
of golden-crested wrens arriving over the sea
that he compared them to a snowstorm, every
bird representing a flake.

One more instance I would give you as to
migration, to show you how attractive it may
be and to show you also how much can be
done in taming birds. In 1921, in my garden,
there were reared two or three broods of
wigeon, which, as you know, is a British duck.
There are some that breed in Scotland, but the
bulk of them go much farther north to breed
and come to us in flocks in autumn and winter.
Three of these birds reared in the garden grew
so tame that they would take food out of my
hand, not snatching it, but continuing to feed
with the bill in the palm of my hand with
complete confidence, though in a wild state
wigeon are very shy birds. Last spring they
went away—two drakes and one duck. Presumably they joined flocks of wild wigeon
going north. They may not have gone far or
they may have gone very far north ; anyhow,
they were away for about seven months. In
November of this year the female bird came
back, and came up to me and began feeding in
exactly the same way out of my hand as she
had done before she went away. About three
weeks afterwards one of the male birds came
back and did exactly the same. It is exceedingly attractive if you can make birds tame so
that, although they may be away amongst
wild birds six or seven months, they yet come

back to the same place, and are as tame as they were before.

Birds have to a greater degree, I think, than any other animate creature, except man, the power to express joy. I will give one or two instances. The flight and song of the lark are familiar to you ; it is a real and evident joy flight. The note of the curlew in spring is a long, vibrating whistle, which is full of joy and very wonderful in expression ; this is uttered mainly in the air, but sometimes partly on the ground. The snipe, too, has a joy flight ; it flies in a wide circuit and, making a short descent from time to time in the air, achieves with the vibration of its tail feathers a noise like the bleating of a goat, which apparently gives the snipe great satisfaction. It will fly round and round for some time continually making that noise, and you cannot watch it without seeing that the flight is an expression of joy.

You have also the family life of birds to consider. Nearly all our British birds are monogamous. There are some exceptions. The black cock—black game—which are indigenous British birds, are polygamous. I do not count the pheasant because the pheasant is not an indigenous bird. He was imported from the East and brought his Eastern customs with him. But most of our birds—the vast majority—are monogamous, and the larger birds—perhaps the smaller ones too—pair for life. I warned you before that when you studied the habits of birds you always found the cuckoo at the discreditable end, and the cuckoo is said to be polyandrous. Though with very few exceptions our birds are all monogamous, in family life they differ. The long-tailed tit's family remain together all through the autumn and winter, sometimes joined by another family. Rooks, of course, live in a community. I think it is not so much family life as life of a community in the case of adult rooks, but with long-tailed tits and part-ridges it is a real family life which is continued after the young birds have grown up until pair-ing time in the next year. Anybody who has had a tame covey of partridges knows how attractive their family life is. The difficulty I have found is that they have never stayed with me after October, they have fallen in with wild birds and left the garden, but a tame covey of partridges, while it remains, is one of the most attractive things I know. That is a high form of family life.

Now consider the robin. He has as little family life as he can. Of course a pair of robins rear their brood each year ; they may even have a second brood, but when the young are able to look after themselves the old birds make the young ones separate from them. And they are not content with that, but the male and female will not spend the autumn and winter together, but each robin has its own territory in which it remains separate and alone through the autumn and winter. If you work in the woods or in the garden you will notice that you are often attended by a robin, but only one at a time, and if another turns up there is a fight between the two. The law of robins apparently is that, except in the actual nesting period, each robin must have one territory, and if another robin comes he or she is breaking the law of robins. This law is as unalterable as that of the Medes and Persians ; it is probably much older and it has certainly lasted much longer. I know of a robin in the nesting season that was so anxious to get food for its young that it acquired a habit of coming on a human hand to get food. It reared two broods this year, and for a time the young were in the same place with it. This robin remains there now and he will come on the hand and sit there and feed, he is so confident. But he never follows you from his own particular territory ; if you want to give him food, you must go to his territory. If you go to another part of the garden some fifty yards away, another robin will come and stand by you, and if you put your hand on the ground he or she (whichever it is) will take something out of your hand. Its habits are quite different from those of the other robin. You never see the two together.

Then again I pass to the discreditable end of the scale and find the cuckoo, which has no family life at all. It is sometimes said that cuckoos exercise a certain kind of superintend-ence over their young that are reared by other birds ; but this is doubtful.

I have taken these instances of birds from common things, because I am trying to show you the sort of pleasure in bird life which anybody that has an interest in birds may find. All the things I have been telling (except the instance of the wigeon, which I admit requires an enclosure with a pond, where things can be kept quiet) are what anybody who lives in the country may notice and enjoy for himself; and they cost nothing. You want really nothing except the power of walking about, good eyesight, and good hearing. Of course, a push bicycle is very useful, far better than a motor-bicycle or a motor-car, which ties you to the roads and makes speed the main object. A push bicycle is a much more subservient thing. It is silent, and it can be wheeled across places where no motor can be taken. A good pair of field-glasses are also useful.

One can go on talking for ever about what has been seen and observed, and it is open to everybody to multiply observations for themselves of things that are within their reach. To tell them is the best way of imparting to, or implanting in, other people something of the pleasure that one has got one's self in bird life or in Outdoor Nature. Of course, Outdoor Nature includes many other things about which I am not qualified to speak. Sir Frederick Keeble, I have no doubt, could tell you the enormous difference it makes in life to take pleasure in wild flowers and have knowledge of them. I have not got that knowledge, but a friend told me the other day that when bicycling near my home with an ordinary hedge on either side of the road, and a wood on part of one side of it, in one half-mile without getting off his bicycle, he counted forty-six different kinds of wild flowers. Think what that half-mile was, from the point of view of interest to my friend, and what an experience of pleasure people may have who know anything about flowers. And it is not only one half-mile that is like this ; it is many half-miles. My friend also told me of a species of buttercup not very rare, but of which in his parish he had at first found only one specimen. Year by year he went to see that specimen flower every April, and it was a pleasure to him. Gradually it increased and multiplied.

And that is another instance that so long as you do not destroy or disturb you can get pleasure in going each year, as my friend did, to see a rare plant flowering in the same place. And every one can do so without spoiling it. The whole world of flowers and trees, of course, can be treated from the same point of view as that of birds. Then there is the whole world of insects—a very gruesome world by all accounts in some respects, but extraordinarily interesting. There is the weather, which may be of the greatest interest. I take great interest in the weather in the country. It is always some sort of a day in the country. The first thing I want to know when I wake up is what sort of a day it is. Take yesterday, the first of

January, a perfect type of one sort of winter
day—sun, a little frost, blue sky, and stillness
the whole day. This morning I woke up to
another sort of day, also attractive, cloudy,
mild, and with that softness in the air which is
a quality of a mild winter day. There you
have two specimens of weather, each to be
enjoyed in its own way, on the first two days
of this year. Then the seasons, and everything which the seasons bring with them.
There is a book, a very remarkable one, written
in German more than sixty years ago, I think,
but translated into English, called " On the
Heights." There is this sentence in it—a
peasant woman and her husband happily
married, living on their own plot of land, and
one day the peasant woman is looking out of
the window at the fruit-trees in the orchard
and she says meditatively, " These are the
trees that blossomed and bore fruit, and then
the snow fell upon them, and then it was spring
again." In that one sentence there is the feeling of outdoor home. You want to be in the
same place, seeing the trees and seeing the
seasons passing over the same trees, seeing the
first tender green of the leaf come out in April
or May, and then seeing the beautiful colour
of it in the autumn, and so you may multiply
pleasure indefinitely. There are the stars, too,
which I have not mentioned, and which have
the advantage that nobody *can* destroy or
disturb them. Surely the Eastern proverb
comes home to us which says " Praise Allah for

the infinite diversity of his handiwork." Books
help you for the study of Outdoor Nature, and
they are very useful in enlarging knowledge,
and by enlarging knowledge you increase
pleasure. For knowledge of the common
English song birds given attractively and
accurately, I recommend Ward Fowler's *A
Year with the Birds* ; and if you want to have
the pleasure of Nature expressed in the best
English you will find this in Walton's *Angler*
and Gilbert White's *Selborne*. There are
also the books of the late Mr. W. H. Hudson.
For knowledge of many things, including the
stars, probably *The Outline of Science*, which
has been coming out in parts and is, I believe,
now complete, will be most valuable. Books
do help, and I would quote to you two stanzas
of Wordsworth which seem to me to have in
them the feeling that I have been trying to
express of the beauty of Nature, of something
which may be a joy to every one. They are
these :

> They dance not for me
> Yet mine is their glee !
> Thus pleasure is spread through the earth,
> In stray gifts to be claimed by whoever shall find,
> And a rich loving kindness, redundantly kind,
> Moves all nature to gladness and mirth.

> The showers of the spring
> Rouse the birds, and they sing ;
> If the wind do but stir for his proper delight,
> Each leaf, that and this, his neighbours will kiss ,
> Each wave, one and t'other, speeds after his brother ;
> They are happy, for that is their right !

That is the "joy in widest commonalty spread."

Joy is not the only aspect of Nature ; but it is the aspect which appeals most to us ; it is a very real one, and I think on the whole the dominating aspect of Outdoor Nature is that of pleasure and joy. There is one sentence from Jeremy Taylor that may be relevant in considering the pleasure that can be got from Outdoor Nature, and it is this : " I sleep, . . . I drink and eat, I read and meditate, I walk in my neighbour's pleasant fields, and see all the varieties of natural beauty, I delight in that in which God delights, that is, in wisdom and virtue, and in the whole creation, and in God himself. And He that hath so many forms of joy, must needs be very much in love with sorrow and peevishness, who loseth all these pleasures, and chooseth to sit upon his little handful of thorns."

I have quoted these things, because I think they have in them the spirit of the pleasure we get from Outdoor Nature if we have the capacity of taking pleasure in it. If people have not that interest in Outdoor Nature—birds, trees, gardens, stars, and all the rest—then let them try to find something else in which they can get as much recreation and pleasure, which is wholesome for the mind and body, and which endures and increases, as does the pleasure in Outdoor Nature for those who have inclination for it. If any one shows signs of that inclination and capacity, I would say to those who

teach him or her, " By all possible means
cultivate that capacity, because if you cultivate
it you will find through life that it goes on
increasing and never palls.   You will be always
getting fresh interest and increasing pleasure,
and in your pleasure you will find happiness
and contentment."

III RECREATION

FALLODON PAPERS

III RECREATION

IT is sometimes said that this is a pleasure-
seeking age. Whether it be a pleasure-
seeking age or not, I doubt whether it is a
pleasure-finding age. We are supposed to have
great advantages in many ways over our pre-
decessors. There is, on the whole, less poverty
and more wealth. There are supposed to be
more opportunities for enjoyment : there are
moving pictures, motor-cars, and many other
things which are now considered means of
enjoyment and which our ancestors did not
possess, but I do not judge from what I read
in the newspapers that there is more content.
Indeed, we seem to be living in an age of
discontent. It seems to be rather on the
increase than otherwise and is a subject of
general complaint. If so it is worth while
considering what it is that makes people happy,
what they can do to make themselves happy,
and it is from that point of view that I wish
to speak on recreation.

Let it be admitted that recreation is only
one of the things that make for happiness in
life. I do not even recommend it as the most

61

important. There are at least four other
things which are more or less under our own
control and which are essential to happiness.
The first is some moral standard by which to
guide our actions. The second is some satisfactory home life in the form of good relations
with family or friends. The third is some form
of work which justifies our existence to our own
country and makes us good citizens. The fourth
thing is some degree of leisure and the use of it
in some way that makes us happy. To succeed
in making a good use of our leisure will not
compensate for failure in any one of the other
three things to which I have referred, but a
reasonable amount of leisure and a good use of
it is an important contribution to a happy life.
How is this happy use of leisure to be ensured ?
We sometimes meet people who do not seem
to know what to do with their spare time.
They are like the man of whom it was said,
" He doesn't know what he wants, and he
won't be happy till he gets it." The first thing,
therefore, is to take ourselves out of that
category, to know definitely what we want,
and to make sure it is something that will
make us happy when we get it ; and that is the
beginning of recreation. You are entitled to
say to me, "That is all very well as a general
piece of advice, but tell us how you have
followed and applied it yourself " ; and it
would not be fair for me to shrink from
answering that question. In one respect I
must plead failure. I have been a failure as

regards golf, not because I did not succeed, but because I did not want to succeed. I have a great respect for golf. I am sure it is very good for many people ; I know very many good people who play golf; but it so happens that it does not give me a good time, and so I leave the recommendation of it to people who can speak of it with more appreciation.

But I do recommend some game or games as a part of recreation. As long as I could see to play and had sufficient leisure, I enjoyed immensely the game of real or court tennis, a very ancient game, requiring activity as well as skill, a game in which Americans may take interest and some pride, because for the first time, at any rate, in the recent history of the game, an amateur is champion of the world and that amateur is an American. The English are sometimes criticized for paying too much attention to games. A British officer whom I know well, who happened to be in Africa at the outbreak of the War and took part in the fighting there, tells me that in one of the German posts captured by the British there was found a map made by the Germans and showing Africa as it was to be when the War was over. The greater part of Africa had become German, and there was nothing left for the British excepting a small patch in the middle of the Sahara Desert which was marked " Footballplatz for the English." Football is a national game in America as well as in England, but I do not suppose that either you or we think that our soldiers fought any worse in the War for having been fond of football. I put games definitely as a desirable part of recreation, and I would say have one or more games of which you are fond, but let them, at any rate in youth, be games which test the wind, the staying power, and the activity of the whole body, as well as skill.

Sport shall be mentioned next. I have had a liking for more than one form of sport, but an actual passion for salmon and trout fishing. Perhaps the following little confidence will give some idea how keen the passion has been. The best salmon and trout fishing in Great Britain ends in September. The best salmon fishing begins again in March. In my opinion the very best of all is to be had in March and April. In October I used to find myself looking forward to salmon fishing in the next March and beginning to spend my spare time thinking about it. I lay awake in bed fishing in imagination the pools which I was not going to see before March at the earliest, till I felt I was spending too much time, not in actual fishing, but in sheer looking forward to it. I made a rule, therefore, that I would not fish pools in imagination before the first of January, so that I might not spend more than two months of spare time in anticipation alone. Salmon fishing as I have enjoyed it, fishing not from a boat, but from one's feet, either on the bank or wading deep in the stream, is a glorious and sustained exercise for the whole body, as well as being an exciting sport ; but many of my friends do not care for it. To them I say, as one who was fond of George Meredith's novels once said to a man who complained that he could not read them, " Why should you ? " If you do not care for fishing, do not fish. Why should you ? But if we are to be quits and you are to be on the same happy level as I have been, then find something for yourself which you like as much as I like fishing.

There are many subjects for recreation. I cannot even mention them all, much less discuss any of them adequately. But I must mention for a high place in recreation the pleasure of gardening, if you are fond of it. Bacon says, " God Almighty first planted a garden, and indeed it is the purest of human pleasures." It is one of those pleasures which follow the law of increasing and not of diminishing returns. The more you develop it and the more you know about it, the more absorbing is the interest of it. There is no season of the year at which the interest ceases and no time of life, so long as sight remains, at which we are too old to enjoy it.

I have now mentioned games, sport, and gardening. No one perhaps has time or opportunity to enjoy all three to the full. A few people may have sufficient range of temperament to care for all three, but many people—I would say most people—who have opportunity may find, at any rate in one of

C

them, something that will contribute to their happiness. I will pass now to a subject which is more important still.

Books are the greatest and the most satisfactory recreation. I mean the use of books for pleasure. Without books, without having acquired the power of reading for pleasure, none of us can be independent, but if we can read we have a sure defence against boredom in solitude. If we have not that defence, we are dependent on the charity of family, friends, or even strangers, to save us from boredom ; but if we can find delight in reading, even a long railway journey alone ceases to be tedious, and long winter evenings to ourselves are an inexhaustible opportunity for pleasure.

Poetry is the greatest literature, and pleasure in poetry is the greatest of literary pleasures. It is also the least easy to attain and there are some people who never do attain it. I met some one the other day who did not care for poetry at all ; it gave her no pleasure, no satisfaction, and only caused her to reflect how much better the thought, so it seemed to her, could be expressed in prose. In the same way there are people who care nothing for music. I knew one Englishman of whom it was said that he knew only two tunes : one was the national anthem, " God Save the King," and the other wasn't. We cannot help these people if they do not care for poetry or music, but I may offer you one or two suggestions founded on my own experience with regard to poetry.

There is much poetry for which most of us do not care, but with a little trouble when we are young we may find one or two poets whose poetry, if we get to know it well, will mean very much to us and become part of ourselves. Poetry does not become intimate to us through the intellect alone ; it comes to us through temperament, one might almost say enters us through the pores of the skin, and it is as if when we get older our skin becomes dry and our temperament hard and we can read only with the head.   It is when we are young, before we reach the age of thirty-five, that we must find out the great poet or poets who have really written specially for us ; and if we are happy enough to find one poet who seems to express things which we have consciously felt in our own personal experience, or to have revealed to us things within ourselves of which we were unconscious until we found them expressed in poetry, we have indeed got a great possession. The love for such poetry which comes to us when we are young will not disappear as we get older ; it will remain in us, becoming an intimate part of our own being, and will be an assured source of strength, consolation, and delight.

There is another branch of literature to which I must make a passing reference : it is that of philosophy. I am bound to refer to it here because I know two men, both of them distinguished in public life, who find real recreation and spend leisure time when they

have it in reading and writing philosophy.
They are both living and I have not their
permission to mention their names, but as I
admire them I mention their recreation, though
with an admiration entirely untinged by envy.
An Oxford professor is alleged to have said
that every one should know enough philosophy to find that he can do without it. I do
not go quite so far as that. When I was an
undergraduate at Oxford, I read Plato because
I was made to read it. After I left Oxford,
I read Plato again to see if I liked it. I did
like it so much that I have never found the
same pleasure in other philosophical writers.
I hope you will not think that I am talking
flippantly. I am talking very seriously—about
recreation, and I feel bound to mention
philosophy in connection with it out of respect
to my friends, but I do not lay much stress
upon it as a means of recreation.

I come now to the main source of literary
recreation in reading : the great books of all
time on which one generation after another has
set the seal of excellence so that we know them
certainly to be worth reading. There is a wide
and varied choice, and it is amongst the old
books that the surest and most lasting recreation is to be found. Some one has said,
"Whenever a new book comes out, read an
old one." We need not take that too literally,
but we should give the old and proved books
the preference. Some one—I think it was
Isaac d'Israeli—said that he who did not make

himself acquainted with the best thoughts of
the greatest writers would one day be mortified
to observe that his best thoughts are their
indifferent ones, and it is from the great books
that have stood the test of time that we shall
get, not only the most lasting pleasure, but a
standard by which to measure our own thoughts,
the thoughts of others, and the excellence of
the literature of our own day. Some years
ago, when I was Secretary for Foreign Affairs
in England, when holidays were often long in
coming, short and precious when they did
come, when work was hard and exhausting
and disagreeable, I found it a good plan when
I got home to my library in the country to have
three books on hand for recreation. One of
them used to be one of those great books of all
time dealing with great events or great thoughts
of past generations. I mention Gibbon's
Decline and Fall of the Roman Empire as an
instance of one such book, which had an atmosphere of greatness into which one passed right
out of the worries of party politics and official
work. Such books take one away to another
world where one finds not only pleasure but
rest. "I like large still books," Tennyson is
reported to have said. And great books not
only give pleasure and rest, but better perspective of the events of our own time. I must
warn you that Gibbon has been called dull. It
is alleged that Sheridan, a man of brilliant wit,
said so, and when a friend reminded him that
in a famous speech he had paid Gibbon the

compliment of speaking of the "luminous page of Gibbon," Sheridan said he must have meant to say "voluminous." If you take the same view of Gibbon, find some other great author whom you do not find dull. There is a host of great writers to choose from. There are plenty of signposts to direct us to old books of interest and value. They have well-known names, and so they stand out and are known like great peaks in mountain ranges of the human intellect.

The second of my books would also be an old book, a novel which had been approved by successive generations. The third would be some modern book, whether serious or light, and in modern books the choice is not so easy. There are many that are excellent, but there are many in which we may find neither pleasure nor profit. If our leisure is short, we have not much time to experiment. The less spare time we have, the more precious it is, and we do not want to waste any of it in experimenting with modern books which we do not find profitable. It is worth while to cultivate a few friends whose intelligence we can respect and whose taste is sympathetic and who read, and to get from them from time to time the names of modern books which they have read and found good. I have had too little time for reading, but that my advice may not be entirely academic I will recommend you, at any rate, one good modern novel. Its name is *The Bent Twig*, the authoress is Dorothy

Canfield, and I can tell you nothing except that she is an American, but the book seems to me one of the best pieces of work in novel-writing that has happened to come under my own observation recently. There are others, no doubt, in plenty, and if you get half a dozen friends who are fond of reading each to recommend you one book as I have done, you will have provision for a little time to come.

To conclude my suggestions about reading, I would urge this. Like all the best things in life, the recreation of reading needs a little planning. When we have a holiday in prospect, we make plans beforehand so that when the time comes we may know exactly where we want to go, what we want to do, how the holiday is to be spent, and have all our prepara-tions ready. If we do not do that, the holiday finds us unprepared and the greater part of it is wasted. So with our spare time, our casual leisure. Do not let it find us unprepared. It is a good plan to make a list of books which, either from our own thought, our own experi-ence, or the recommendation of friends, we feel a desire to read. We should have one or two of these books always at hand, and have them in mind, too, as something which we are longing to read at the first opportunity. I think some people lose the habit and pleasure of reading because they do not take this trouble and make no plan, and when the spare evening or the long railway journey or the wet day comes, it finds them without any book in anticipation, and they pick up a newspaper or a magazine, not because they specially want to read it, but because they have nothing present to their minds or at hand which they really care for. The habit of planning ahead is essential to real cultivation of the pleasure of reading, just as essential as planning is for sport or travel or games or any of the other pleasures of life. I know friends who are fond of sport. They choose a long time beforehand the river they will fish or the sort of shooting they will pursue. Another friend likes travel, and plans months in advance where he will go and what he will see. Without this forethought and planning, they would not get their pleasure ; and so it is with reading. If we once acquire the habit of planning, we find out increasingly what it is that we like, and our difficulty at any spare moment is not to find some book that we are longing to read, but to choose which book of those to which we are looking forward in anticipation we shall take first.

I have spoken about planning for a holiday, and I will give an instance of how thoroughly President Roosevelt planned for a holiday. Several years ago when I was at the Foreign Office in London, I got a letter from Mr. Bryce, who was then British Ambassador at Washington, saying that President Roosevelt intended to travel as soon as he was out of office. He was going to travel in Africa, to visit Europe, and to come to England, and he was planning his holiday so minutely as to time his visit to

England for the spring, when the birds would be in full song and hè could hear them. For this purpose he wanted it to be arranged that somebody who knew the songs of the English birds should go for a walk with him in the country, and as the songs were heard tell him what the birds were. That is a pretty good instance of thorough planning in advance for a holiday. It seemed to me very attractive that the executive head of the most powerful country in the world should have this simple, healthy, touching desire to hear the songs of birds, and I wrote back at once to Mr. Bryce to say that when President Roosevelt came to England I should be delighted to do for him what he wanted. It is no more a necessary qualification for the Secretary for Foreign Affairs in London than it is for the President of the United States that he should know the songs of the birds, and it is an amusing coincidence that we should have been able to arrange this little matter satisfactorily between us as if it were part of our official duties, without feeling obliged to call in experts.

Time passed, and when the President retired from office he went to Africa and had much big-game shooting and travel there. Then he came by way of the Sudan and Egypt to Europe. The leading countries of Europe were stirred to do him honour, England not less than others. He had a great reception and everywhere a programme of great and dignified character was arranged for him. European newspapers

were full of it long before he got to England,
and I thought this little walk to hear the songs
of English birds suggested some two years
previously would be forgotten and crowded
out by greater matters. But it was not so.
Without any reminder on my part, I got an
intimation from the English friend who was to
be Colonel Roosevelt's host in London that
Colonel Roosevelt had written to him to say
that this promise had been made and that he
wished time to be found for the fulfilment of it.
I saw Colonel Roosevelt once soon after he
came to London. The day was arranged and
at the appointed time we met at Waterloo
Station. We had to ask the newspaper
reporters not to go with us—not because it
made any difference to Colonel Roosevelt,
but because birds are not so tame, or perhaps
I should say are more self-conscious than public
men and do not like to be photographed or
even interviewed at close quarters, and it
was necessary, not only that Colonel Roosevelt
and I should be alone, but that we should make
ourselves as inconspicuous and unobtrusive as
possible.

So we went alone, and for some twenty hours
we were lost to the world. We went by train
to a country station where a motor was await-
ing us. Thence we drove to the little village
of Titchborne in Hampshire, and got there soon
after midday. In the village of Titchborne
there lives also the family of Titchborne, and
in the old village church there is a tomb with

recumbent figures of one of the Titchbornes
and his wife who lived in the time of James the
First ; on it is inscribed the statement that he
chose to be buried with his wife in this chapel,
which was built by his ancestor in the time of
Henry the First. That shows a continuous
record of one family in one place for some eight
hundred years. I forget whether we had time
to go into the church and look at it, but the
songs of the birds which we had come to hear
are far more ancient. There must be the same
songs that were heard by the inhabitants of
England before the Romans came, for the songs
of birds come down unchanged through great
antiquity, and we are listening to-day, in
whatever part of the world we may be, to
songs which must have been familiar to races
of men of which history has no knowledge and
no record.

I was a little apprehensive about this walk.
I had had no personal acquaintance with
Colonel Roosevelt before he came to England
in 1910, and I thought to myself, " Perhaps,
after all, he will not care so very much about
birds, and possibly after an hour or so he will
have had enough of them. If that be so and he
does not care for birds, he will have nothing
but my society, which he will not find suffi-
ciently interesting for so long a time." I had
relied upon the birds to provide entertainment
for him. If that failed, I doubted my own
resources. I need have had no fear about his
liking for birds. I found, not only that he had

a remarkable and abiding interest in birds,
but a wonderful knowledge of them. Though I
know something about British birds, I should
have been lost and confused among American
birds, of which unhappily I know little or
nothing. Colonel Roosevelt not only knew
more about American birds than I did about
British birds, but he knew about British birds
also. What he had lacked was an opportunity
of hearing their songs, and you cannot get a
knowledge of the songs of birds in any other
way than by listening to them.

We began our walk, and when a song was
heard, I told him the name of the bird. I
noticed that as soon as I mentioned the name,
it was unnecessary to tell him more. He knew
what the bird was like. It was not necessary
for him to see it. He knew the kind of bird
it was, its habits and appearance. He just
wanted to complete his knowledge by hearing
the song. He had, too, a very trained ear for
bird songs, which cannot be acquired without
having spent much time in listening to them.
How he had found time in that busy life to
acquire this knowledge so thoroughly it is
almost impossible to imagine, but there the
knowledge and training undoubtedly were. He
had one of the most perfectly trained ears for
bird songs that I have ever known, so that if
three or four birds were singing together he
would pick out their songs, distinguish each,
and ask to be told each separate name ; and
when, farther on, we heard any bird for a

second time, he would remember the song from the first telling and be able to name the bird himself.

He had not only a trained ear, but keen feeling and taste for bird songs. He was quick to express preferences, and at once picked out the song of the English blackbird as being the best of the bird songs we heard. I have always had the same feeling about the blackbird's song. I do not say it is better than the songs of American birds, which I have not heard, and I think Colonel Roosevelt thought one or two of the American bird songs were better than anything we had in England ; but his feeling for the English blackbird's song I found confirmed the other day in a book published by Dr. Chapman, of the Natural History Museum at New York. He has written a chapter on English birds, and picks out the song of the blackbird for excellence because of its "spiritual quality." Colonel Roosevelt liked the song of the blackbird so much that he was almost indignant that he had not heard more of its reputation before. He said everybody talked about the song of the thrush ; it had a great reputation, but the song of the blackbird, though less often mentioned, was much better than that of the thrush. He wanted to know the reason of this injustice and kept asking the question of himself and me. At last he suggested that the name of the bird must have injured its reputation. I suppose the real reason is that the thrush sings for a longer period of the year than the black-bird and is a more obtrusive singer, and that so few people have sufficient feeling about bird songs to care to discriminate.

One more instance I will give of his interest and his knowledge. We were passing under a fir-tree when we heard a small song in the tree above us. We stopped, and I said that was the song of a golden-crested wren. He listened very attentively while the bird repeated its little song, as its habit is. Then he said, " I think that is exactly the same song as that of a bird that we have in America " ; and that was the only English song that he recognized as being the same as any bird song in America. Some time afterward I met a bird expert in the Natural History Museum in London and told him this incident, and he confirmed what Colonel Roosevelt had said, that the song of this bird would be about the only song that the two countries had in common. I think that a very remarkable instance of minute and accurate knowledge on the part of Colonel Roosevelt. It was the business of the bird expert in London to know about birds. Colonel Roosevelt's knowledge was a mere incident acquired, not as part of the work of his life, but entirely outside it. I remember thinking at the time how strange it seemed that the golden-crested wren, which is the very smallest bird which we have in England, should be the only song bird which the great continent of North America has in common with us.

But points of view are different in different countries. We may find ourselves looking, not only at political questions, but at incidents in natural history, from a different point of view when we are on different sides of an ocean. The other day I was in a contemplative mood not far from Washington. I was thinking what a great country I was in, how much larger the rivers were and how vast the distances, and generally working up in my own mind an impression of the great size of the country. Then I happened to recall this incident of the golden-crested wren, and I found myself thinking, of course, in a tiny little island like Great Britain, where one cannot go in an express train at fifty miles an hour from east to west or from north to south in a straight line for more than fifteen hours without falling into the sea, the only song we could have in common with a great continent like this would be the song of the smallest bird.

One trivial incident there was in our walk which gave us some amusement. We were going by footpaths down a river valley, a very beautiful, but a very tame and settled country, where anything like an adventure seemed impossible. We were on a path which I had known for many years, and along which I had walked many times, not only without adventure, but without even incident. Suddenly we found ourselves stopped—the path was flooded, some weeds had blocked the river close by, and instead of a dry path we had about twenty

yards of water in front of us. The water was
not very deep, certainly not above our knees,
but I had not intended that there should be
any wading in our walk nor had I prepared for
it. I asked if he would mind going through the
water, to which, of course, he replied that he
would not. So we went through, got wet, and
in the course of the afternoon got dry again
as we walked. Nothing of the same kind had
happened there before ; nothing has happened
since. I think there was some magnetism
about Colonel Roosevelt's personality which
created incidents.

After going a few miles down the valley, we
got into our motor, which was waiting at a
village inn, and drove to what is called the
New Forest, though it is more than eight
hundred years old. We were now in a country
of wild heath, quite uncultivated, and the part
we went through was mostly natural forest.
Here we heard some birds different from any
we had heard in the valley of the Itchen, and
got to a little inn standing on the open heath
about nine o'clock in the evening. We had
dinner, and next morning we breakfasted
together and went to Southampton, whence
Colonel Roosevelt returned to America.

I am not attempting here a full appreciation
of Colonel Roosevelt. He will be known for all
time as one of the great men of America. I am
only giving you this personal recollection as a
little contribution to his memory, as one that
I can make from personal knowledge and which

is now known only to myself. His conversation about birds was made interesting by quotations from poets. He talked also about politics, and in the whole of his conversation about them there was nothing but the motive of public spirit and patriotism. I saw enough of him to know that to be with him was to be stimulated in the best sense of the word for the work of life. Perhaps it is not yet realized how great he was in the matter of knowledge as well as in action. Everybody knows that he was a great man of action in the fullest sense of the word. The Press has always proclaimed this. It is less often that a tribute is paid to him as a man of knowledge as well as a man of action. Two of your greatest experts in natural history told me the other day that Colonel Roosevelt could, in that department of knowledge, hold his own with experts. His knowledge of literature was also very great, and it was knowledge of the best. It is seldom that you find so great a man of action who was also a man of such wide and accurate knowledge. I happened to be impressed by his knowledge of natural history and literature and to have had first-hand evidence of both, but I gather from others that there were other fields of knowledge in which he was also remarkable. Not long ago when an English friend of mine was dying, his business agent came over to see him. One of the family asked the agent whether he had come on important business. " No," he said, " I have come for a little con-

versation because I was feeling depressed this
morning and I wanted to be made to feel two
inches taller." That saying would, I think,
have been specially applicable to Colonel
Roosevelt also. He could make people feel
bigger and stronger and better.

And now my last discourse shall be on one
sentence from Colonel Roosevelt which I saw
quoted the other day. It is this : " He is not
fit to live who is not fit to die, and he is not fit
to die who shrinks from the joy of life or from
the duty of life." Observe that the joy of life
and the duty of life are put side by side. Many
people preach the doctrine of the duty of life.
It is comparatively seldom that you find one
who puts the joy of life as something to be
cultivated, to be encouraged on an equal foot-
ing with the duty of life. And of all the joys
of life which may fairly come under the head
of recreation there is nothing more great, more
refreshing, more beneficial in the widest sense
of the word, than a real love of the beauty of
the world. Some people cannot feel it. To
such people I can only say, as Turner once said
to a lady who complained that she could not
see sunsets as he painted them, " Don't you
wish you could, madam ? " But to those who
have some feeling that the natural world has
beauty in it I would say, Cultivate this feeling
and encourage it in every way you can. Consider the seasons, the joy of the spring, the
splendour of the summer, the sunset colours
of the autumn, the delicate and graceful bare-

ness of winter trees, the beauty of snow, the beauty of light upon water, what the old Greek called the unnumbered smiling of the sea.

In the feeling for that beauty, if we have it, we possess a pearl of great price. I say of great price, but it is something which costs us nothing because it is all a part of the joy which is in the world for everybody who cares for it. It is the "joy in widest commonalty spread"; it is a rich possession for us if we care for it, but in possessing it we deprive nobody else. The enjoyment of it, the possession of it, excites neither greed nor envy, and it is something which is always there for us and which may take us out of the small worries of life. When we are bored, when we are out of tune, when we have little worries, it clears our feelings and changes our mood if we can get in touch with the beauty of the natural world. There is a quaint but apposite quotation from an old writer which runs as follows : "I sleep, I drink and eat, I read and meditate, I walk in my neighbour's pleasant fields and see all the varieties of natural beauty . . . and he who hath so many forms of joy must needs be very much in love with sorrows and peevishness, who loseth all these pleasures and chooseth to sit upon his little handful of thorns."

There is a story of a man whom others called poor, and who had just enough fortune to support himself in going about the country in the simplest way and studying and enjoying the life and beauty of it. He was once in the

company of a great millionaire who was engaged
in business, working at it daily and getting
richer every year, and the poor man said to the
millionaire, " I am a richer man than you are."
" How do you make that out ? " said the
millionaire. " Why," he replied, " I have got
as much money as I want and you haven't."

But it is not only in the small worries of life
that we may be saved by a right use of recreation. We all realize how in the Great War
your nation and our nation and others engaged
in the War were taken out of themselves, I was
going to say lost themselves, but I ought rather
to say found themselves. It was a fine thing
on your part to send two million soldiers across
the sea in so short a time to risk their lives for
an ideal. It was even more impressive to us
when we heard that in this country you had
adopted conscription, and that your millions
of people, distributed over so vast an extent of
continent, were so moved by one public spirit
and one patriotism and one desire to help the
Allies in the War that they were rationing
themselves voluntarily with food and fuel.
That voluntary action by so many millions
over so great an extent of country was a
tremendous example, showing what an ideal
and a public spirit and a call to action can do
for people in making them forget private interests and convenience and making them great.

That was an example of what could be done
by not shrinking from the duty of life ; but you
can get greatness, too, from some of the joys

of life, and from none more than from a keen
sense of the beauty of the world and a love
for it. I found it so during the War. Our
feelings were indeed roused by the heroism of
our people, but they were also depressed by
the suffering. In England every village was
stricken, there was grief in almost every house.
The thought of the suffering, the anxiety for
the future, destroyed all pleasure. It came
even between one's self and the page of the
book one tried to read. In those dark days I
found some support in the steady progress
unchanged of the beauty of the seasons. Every
year, as spring came back unfailing and un-
faltering, the leaves came out with the same
tender green, the birds sang, the flowers came
up and opened, and I felt that a great power of
Nature for beauty was not affected by the War.
It was like a great sanctuary into which we
could go and find refuge for a time from even
the greatest trouble of the world, finding there
not enervating ease, but something which gave
optimism, confidence, and security. The progress of the seasons unchecked, the continu-
ance of the beauty of Nature, was a manifesta-
tion of something great and splendid which not
all the crimes and follies and misfortunes of
mankind can abolish or destroy. If, as years
go on, we can feel the beauty of the world as
Wordsworth felt it, and get from it

> Authentic tidings of invisible things,
> Of ebb and flow and ever during power,
> And central peace subsisting at the heart
> Of endless agitation,

then we have, indeed, a recreation which will
give us, not merely pleasure, but strength,
refreshment, and confidence. Something of
the same feeling we may get from an appreciation of great music, beautiful pictures, splendid
architecture, and other things that stir us with
an impression of everlasting greatness. Enjoy
these and cultivate the appreciation of them,
but especially, if you can, cultivate the enjoyment of the beauty of Nature, because it costs
nothing and is everywhere for everybody ; and
if we can find recreation in such things as
these, then, indeed, we may make the joy of
life great as well as the duty of life, and we
may find that the joy of life and the duty of
life are not things adverse or even to be con-
trasted, but may be, as Colonel Roosevelt puts
them, companions and complements of each
other.

IV SOME THOUGHTS ON PUBLIC LIFE

IV SOME THOUGHTS ON PUBLIC LIFE

TO begin with, I would look back to the
time when I first entered public life,
not in order that I may praise the " good old
times " or suggest that we should go back to
them, but because a good many people have
considerable difficulty at present in knowing
exactly where we are. And one way to help in
ascertaining where we are is to look back on
the road by which we have travelled to the
point we have now reached. When I first took
part in political life, in 1884, politics were much
simpler than they are now. The dominating
question at that particular election which
followed soon afterward was the simple question of the extension of the franchise to the
counties. There were, it is true, other political
questions, but that was the one which dominated that election. It was, in other words,
the completing of the establishment of representative government based upon household
suffrage. The issue was so simple that there
was no distinction between Liberals and
Labour. Men like Mr. Burt and Mr. Fenwick,
who were as truly Labour men as any Labour

representative of the present day, belonging to, and coming to Parliament direct from, the class of wage-earners, were as much members of the Liberal Party as any one else. They were offered, and they accepted, membership of the Liberal Party on precisely the same terms and conditions as other Liberal politicians. The issue was very simple, and, putting aside the Irish Party, there were only two great Parties —Liberal and Conservative—the Liberal Party having Labour members amongst it. We did not ask many questions ; at any rate, not so many as we do now. It was assumed that if the Government was established on a real representative basis, all the shortcomings of which the country might have been conscious under previous less representative systems of government would find a remedy.

The first thing which occurred to us soon afterward was that the shortcomings which were really due to previous systems of government did not entirely coincide with the short-comings which were thought to be due to them. The things which were due to them were no doubt remedied by the more democratic representative government ; but there remained many things, which were thought to be due to previous systems of government, which were, in fact, due to other causes.

At that time no one questioned that democratic representative parliamentary government was the best form of government, and that as far as any government could do it, it would satisfy the needs of the community. Where do we stand to-day? When I entered political life it was the latter part of the epoch of the establishment of democratic representative government. We have lived on to-day into an epoch which regards democratic representative government as on its trial. Its merits and efficiency are questioned as they were not questioned when we were engaged in establishing it. In some countries democratic representative government is no longer regarded as an ideal at all. I do not take what has happened in Russia as an instance, because Russia has never had representative government, and what has never had a trial cannot be said to be superseded or discarded by what has taken place in Russia. But what has happened in Italy lately is very significant. Italy had democratic representative government, but it has now been superseded by something which presumably must have much popular support behind it, but which is not based upon parliamentary election, but on organized force. For the present, at any rate, that system of government which we have regarded as the ideal in this country has been suspended in Italy; and it is possible that under the shock of confusion and chaos that still exists in Europe you may see democratic representative government in some other countries go down, at any rate for a time, in favour of some other system.

There are many people to-day who question

the efficacy of democratic representative government in a way that it has never been questioned before. Personally, I remain as attached
to democratic representative government as I
have ever been. I am not going over a long
list of achievements under that system, such as
development of education, the rise in the
general standard of life, and the securing of
impartial administration of justice—a long list
might be given under which democratic representative government, compared with systems
which preceded it, must be pronounced a great
success. But there are people who judge it,
not by the standard of what preceded it, but
by the standard of what they think ought to be
done ; and it is possible to argue, at any rate
as regards some things which have been done
in recent years under democratic representative government, that they might have been
accomplished under some other system.

There is, however, one thing which I believe
to be indisputable—it is this : that under
democratic representative government we are
enjoying the greatest amount of individual
personal liberty that has ever been enjoyed in
any country. I was once present at a conversation in the United States between two people,
both of experience and intelligence, who were
comparing life in the United States with life
in Great Britain. One of them said : " What
I like in the United States is the entire absence
of all class feeling ; in England, there are the
old class traditions, the barriers of reserve, and

there is still, though less than there used to be, a considerable amount of class feeling. In the United States some people are richer than others, but there is not the same consciousness of class differences ; there is a sense of everybody meeting as equals with a frankness and absence of embarrassment or reserve which I find exceedingly refreshing." (My own short experience of the United States made me feel this too.) The other man said : " That is true ; but, on the other hand, there is in the United States more executive interference with personal liberty than there is in Great Britain, and American people here are more tolerant of that interference." I cannot of my own knowledge express an opinion on this point ; but the conversation interested me, and set me thinking— to what is our personal liberty in this country really due, and what is its chief guaranty ? It seems to me that its great guaranty is this : that not only have we a government elected by popular vote, but dependent from day to day, when Parliament is sitting, upon the confidence of the representatives of the people in the House of Commons : if anything occurs in this country which is regarded as an undue interference with personal liberty of individuals of whatever class, or if anything occurs which outrages our sense of fairness, it is known that either the government must put that right or cease to exist. The daily responsibility, when Parliament is sitting, of the government to the elected representatives of the people is, I consider, our great guaranty of personal liberty. I cannot imagine any other system of government which would not interfere with personal liberty to a much greater extent than the system we now have. It is possible to argue that we might gain certain advantages by some other system of government, but I am sure the price we should have to pay would be that of submitting to much greater interference with personal liberty than under the system we have at present. This asset of personal liberty is so great that whatever shortcomings there may be in the present system, I prefer the ills of the present to the ills of any other system, which would impose new and stringent restrictions on personal liberty.

I am, therefore, examining shortcomings, not with the object of showing that democratic representative government is something that could with advantage be superseded or replaced, but to consider how best it can be strengthened and improved. One of the things to beware of in democratic representative government is reliance upon a formula which may not be based on a sound premise. There is no more pleasing formula than that of "government of the people, by the people, for the people." In Abraham Lincoln's great speech it had a magnificent place. But it is well not to use that formula too confidently. It presupposes that the people are both willing and capable of governing. If they are not willing and capable of governing, the formula

has no value. In the same way, consider
" government by public opinion " as a formula.
Public opinion—that highest tribunal with
which I have heard leaders of opposition
threaten governments in the House of Commons. It is an admirable formula ; but it
presupposes not only that public opinion exists,
but that on any particular question there is
a public opinion ready to decide the issue.
Indeed, it presupposes that the supreme states-
man in democratic government is public
opinion. Many of the shortcomings of democratic government are due to the fact that
public opinion is not necessarily a great states-
man at all.

For example, I will take the history over a
long series of years of our dealings with Ireland.
For a long time there was practically no public
opinion about Ireland. It knew nothing about
and was not interested in Ireland. That was
not statesmanlike. Many of the evils of British
government in Ireland were due to that. Then
one of the great English parties adopted Home
Rule, and public opinion did become very
interested indeed in Ireland. But it was so
divided that as a matter of fact it did not make
it possible for any policy to be consistently
pursued. I dare say historians of the future
will find fault with the want of statesmanship
in British dealings with Ireland, and they will
find fault with statesmen : but the real fault
was, I think, with public opinion. The Home
Ruler will hold that if there had been a suffi-

ciently overwhelming public opinion to make
Mr. Gladstone's Home Rule measure prevail
in 1886, Irish difficulties would have been
solved. Unionists, on the other hand, will
hold that if only public opinion had been
solid in supporting the policy of Lord Salisbury
and Mr. Balfour, and in giving no countenance
to Home Rule, the Irish problems would have
been solved in that way. The answer of both
Mr. Gladstone and Lord Salisbury might well
be : that each believed in his own policy for
Ireland, but that neither of them had had a
real chance to give effect to his policy. Either
might have been right or either might have
been wrong. But public opinion was so divided
that neither policy was given a sufficient chance
of success. That is want of statesmanship in
public opinion.

It is true that a definite policy towards
Ireland has been adopted now, but I think
public opinion acquiesced in it rather than
approved it. I am not thinking of criticizing
it. But I do think that public opinion
acquiesced in that settlement, not so much
as an act of statesmanship or of considered
opinion as from passive acquiescence due to
sheer exhaustion. If that be so, it leads to this
reflection : that in a democratic representative
government we want statesmanship, and the
only secure basis of statesmanship is that
public opinion should be statesmanlike.

That carries me a little farther to another
reflection. In those years—from 1885 to 1914

—the great dividing issues between parties were the extension of the franchise to the counties, Irish Home Rule, and Tariff Reform. These three questions were purely political questions ; that is to say, they could be carried into operation by Act of Parliament, by a stroke of the parliamentary pen, and could have been put into operation in no other way. That alone made the problem comparatively simple and entirely one for political parties.

But, now, what is the most important domestic question in our public affairs at the present moment ? I should say it is the relations between Capital and Labour—between employers and employed. It transcends in importance all questions of domestic politics. How far is this a political question in the sense of being one to be solved by parties in the House of Commons ? If you hold that the solution is the destruction of private enterprise, the nationalization of great industries, of course it is a political question to be settled by Parliament. But I think the majority of people, deeply impressed as they are by the fact that relations between Capital and Labour are not satisfactory, are not yet of opinion that nationalization would make things better ; and although they are convinced that there ought to be and must be a change, they are looking for the change in other directions. Now, in what direction ? I read the other day a book, evidently written with knowledge and with a sincere desire to be impartial, on the subject

D

of what the great mass of organized labour really most desires. What are the points which are at the moment causing the most interest and anxiety amongst the wage-earning classes? I give them in the order stated by the writer as that in which they are felt by wage-earners to be most urgent and important to themselves.

The first is security against unemployment —not merely to relieve present unemployment, but to give security against it in the future. The writer had gathered from the wage-earners themselves that, if they could have security against the apprehension that their employment might not be permanent, it would be regarded by them as one of the greatest assets they could obtain.

Well, I believe the best way of dealing with that point, the most helpful way of dealing with it, with the minimum of waste and the avoidance of abuse, combined with the maximum of efficiency, would be a real insurance against unemployment in the great trades themselves. I do not want to argue the merits of this. My point is that if this be so, though government may assist, it is in the main something that must be worked out by employers and employed acting together.

Second, the writer puts the status of the worker. The wage-earners, he said, resent having no share in the businesses, and not merely no share in the management, but they resent the feeling that all arrangements for carrying on the business which affects their daily life are made solely with reference to the convenience of the employer, without the workers being considered or given any share in the ordering of the work. That is to say, the workers desire to be regarded not as mere parts of a machine, but as something to be consulted in the working of that machine.

That is a difficult question. I do not believe that Parliament could settle it satisfactorily. It is a most important question ; but it can be dealt with, and must be dealt with, by good-will and statesmanship on the part of employers and employed, dealing with each other direct, and not by the indirect route of Parliament.

Third, the writer puts the question of wages —that the workers should get the maximum share that is possible out of the profits of the industry. That again is a question which I do not believe can be settled by the State, but must be settled by employers and employed ; that is to say, by the great organized bodies of employers and the great organized bodies of labour consulting together.

These questions, which are of vital import- ance, are questions that require great states- manship, just as much statesmanship as is required in dealing with problems in Parlia- ment, but the statesmanship will have to be applied direct by the people concerned them- selves. In democracy there is more than ever need for statesmanship : and if democracy is

to work well in dealing with many problems
which could not be dealt with adequately
through parliamentary representatives, the
people most concerned must apply that statesmanship direct in dealing with their own
problems.

Having arrived at this point, that there is a
great need for more statesmanship in public
opinion, let us ask, What is the remedy ? The
true answer, I believe, is in the word " education." Not primary, not secondary, but adult
education, the education which the people give
themselves after they have got past the best
primary and secondary education they can get.
In other words, it is the bringing of university
education within reach of those who have had
secondary education and are now engaged in
various professions and other walks of life.
I am told that there is an immense demand for
that form of education : that there is a real
thirst for it, such as has hitherto been un-
known. If that is so, it is a demand that
should be met, and happily, it is one that can
be met. It has the advantage over primary
and secondary education, in that it costs
infinitely less in money to bring a good university education within the reach of those who
wish to take advantage of it—because you do
not require a vast outlay on new school build-
ings and the cost of maintaining such, which is
necessary for primary or secondary education.
I am told that £500,000 a year would do an
enormous amount in this way for people who

realize that the education that really becomes part of a man or woman's self is the education that they seek and find themselves, when they are grown up. Five hundred thousand pounds a year would do an immense national service in this way.

Another great source of education is the press. My own unfortunate disability of sight prevents me from being able to make extensive reading of the press. But from what reading I do make, I find it very easy to get very much admirable information in the press, and to find leading articles which, whether or not I agree with the particular conclusions, are evidently written with knowledge, thought, and force. If you have any criticism to make on the press, I think the answer of the press would be this : those who control the press study the circulation of their papers ; people can have the sort of press they deserve, and it rests with the people themselves. As I have said, from my own experience, you can to-day get excellent education from the press, and it rests with the people themselves to secure and read the newspapers where it is to be found.

A third source of education is the politicians themselves. I have no sympathy with the abuse of politicians. I would say again, that the people get the politicians they deserve. The remedy is in their own hands. I would make only this one point on this subject. There is too much tendency (take the literature which is issued at political elections, for example) to talk down to people unnecessarily, instead of expecting people to come up to a higher level. I have seen political leaflets— I won't say from which party they came—that seemed to be written on the assumption that the average elector was childish, absolutely ignorant, and entirely selfish. I think that political literature or speeches which under-estimate the mental or moral level of the community are simply so much waste. They do not get real response from democracy : a great response is given only to an appeal to the higher and not the lower instincts and feelings of the community.

This was brought to my mind in strong and convincing manner by having the good fortune during the War to have many conversations with the late Mr. Page, who was American Ambassador to this country. What an inestim-able debt this country owes to him it is now beginning to understand ! I cannot here review his career, or enter upon an extensive eulogy of Mr. Page ; there was no man for whom I came to have a greater admiration and personal regard, but I can only tell you to-day two things which impressed me specially about him, and which occur to me now as being specially relevant to the point I desire to make.

One was his intense feeling for right against wrong. Once he became sensible that a moral issue was involved, from that moment right or wrong was the supreme test with him. It decided his opinion absolutely, and made him on that particular issue have all the conviction, the fervour, the energy that a man has who is possessed with strong views on the question of religion. The other point was this : that having convinced himself on what was right, nothing would shake his belief that if a great democracy, especially his own American democracy, was appealed to on a vital question in a great manner, it would most certainly respond. If a democracy did not respond to a great appeal, his view was, not that the appeal was above their heads, but that the appeal had not been lofty enough. If only it was great, lofty, and noble, his faith was that democracy, when so appealed to, would rise and respond. I never met any one who made me feel so certain that his trust in the people was sincere, deep, and unshakable. The late Mr. Page was a man who really did trust the people. I regarded him as the most convinced believer in democracy that I have ever known. These two qualities of Mr. Page I have referred to as being qualities upon which politicians, I think, could rely more than they do, and which they should particularly encourage and cultivate.

To sum up the past, I would observe that one of the great dangers in democracy is the lack of interest, lethargy, and therefore absence of public opinion. There is no better, no more certain corrective of this than to make it clear that moral issues are involved. Once that is made clear, the public interest is certainly aroused. The other danger is the great activity on the part of a section of public opinion, an activity which is ill-informed and therefore misdirected, an activity which is based on the assumption that they know everything, when as a matter of fact they may know very little. The greatest corrective of that is education, particularly adult education.

One factor no doubt in interesting democracy, in making public opinion vital, is to have in public life striking personalities. It is not enough that there should be only ideas, knowledge, and principles : there must be strong and vivid personalities. The history of all religions is an illustration of what I mean. Moral principles have always been something of which different generations of men have been aware : but there comes at certain great epochs in human history some great person in whom these great principles are embodied, and they at once become vital and living, moving masses of mankind in a way they have not done before. I am not thinking merely of Christianity, but of all great religious movements, such as Mohammedanism, Buddhism, and Confucianism. You find behind these great movements a great personality.

So in our public affairs we want personalities who are striking and interesting, and who become the embodiment of fine and lofty ideas. There is indeed this danger, that a democracy may set too high a premium upon the gift of public speaking. The public man becomes

interesting by the gift of public speaking, and
we are apt to overestimate people through
admiration of the excellence of their speech.
Cogency of language, as we listen to it, makes
us feel that there must be behind it knowledge,
firmness, a lofty moral purpose—all the great
qualities that we want a man to possess—but it
does not follow that those things are behind
the gift of speech.   Sometimes, one thinks that
in a democracy the gift of public speech has
an undue advantage over other qualities, and
that democracy is likely to be led away and
to mistake some of the smaller men for the
greater men, and to ignore some of the greater
men who may not have the same gift of elo-
quence.   I do not think that danger is so great
as might be supposed.   I think it was Wordsworth who, toward the end of the eighteenth
century, after hearing some of the great
speakers in Parliament of that day, said that
" he came away from listening to Burke with
his head full ; from listening to Fox with his
feelings excited ; and from listening to Pitt
with astonishment at his power to make the
worse appear the better reason."

But there are many men who have qualities
greater than their gift of speech.   The late
Mr. Thomas Burt was an excellent speaker ;
yet there were many other excellent speakers,
some of them more effective than he in making
an audience cheer, who never attained the
same influence in public life.   The reason was
this : that Mr. Burt's ascendancy was due not

so much to his gift of speech, in which he did
not surpass some others, as to the character,
sincerity, wide knowledge, and range of mind
which informed his speech. And so in the long
run I do believe that, though for public life
a certain gift of speech is necessary, the man
with character and wide understanding of
human problems will win in the end, as against
the man with remarkable gifts of speech, but
deficient in character or real ability of thought
and understanding.

Another point worth considering—besides
the effect of public men on public life—is the
effect of public life on public men. Most of us
are people of mixed motives. For instance,
when we begin to prepare a speech, we may
think solely of the merits of our subject ; but
before we come to deliver our speech there will
have crept into it things which have been
prompted by a desire to please and to succeed.
It is quite right that there should be some such
things in every speech. The late Professor
Jowett (I do not know if it is true) is said to
have advised a man, when writing, to read his
manuscript carefully and to strike out anything
that struck him as being particularly fine. You
could not apply that to public speaking ;
nobody would listen. I remember an amusing
story (told, I think, by Mr. Bernard Shaw) of a
man who was a keen politician but a bad
speaker. His imperfections in this respect
were counterbalanced by excellence in playing
the concertina. In order to collect a crowd at

the street corner, he would play his concertina. When he spoke, the audience gradually diminished. His concertina was then brought into play again, and the crowd would again collect. In this way he sought to get his points brought home to the people. It is legitimate, with most of us it is even necessary, that in our speeches there should be a certain amount of concertina playing, if we are fortunate enough to have any gift for playing it.

As to mixed motives, I would credit a parliamentary candidate with three motives, namely, (1) A desire to serve the interests of the country ; (2) a desire to serve the interests of his party, believing that this was the most practical form in which to achieve the former object ; (3) a desire for personal success, which may be a legitimate, indeed wholesome motive, provided it is kept within bounds ; because with the ordinary man—I am not speaking of rare idealists—the desire for personal success greatly facilitates his work and helps him to get hard work out of himself. But that desire has its dangers. The tendency is, in the long run, for a man's views of public life to be decided not by the interest of the country, but by the desire for personal success, which at the beginning is to be regarded as a useful stimulus, but which is not the highest, and should never become the dominant, motive. There is a law, I believe, in currency, which says that if good money and bad money are put into circulation together, the bad money drives out the good.

And there is a tendency for the inferior motive to drive out the superior motive in a man's character.

The sound advice, therefore, to a young man entering public life, is to watch his motives, to watch them constantly and carefully. In public life, if all secrets were known, we should probably find in the record of public men a considerable proportion who started their life with high motives and ended it dominated by smaller ones. I would say, watch your motives, be honest with yourselves about your motives. That, I believe, is one of the most important rules for any man to observe in dealing with public affairs, and indeed in all the conduct of his life.

It was said once that there were seven wise men in Greece, who gained their reputation by their wise sayings. One of them apparently contributed greatly to his reputation by the saying : " Know thyself." I used to think that he got his reputation cheaply. I am convinced now that there is a very large number of people who do not know themselves, and I am quite certain from my own experience that, instead of being easy, it is exceedingly difficult to know oneself. The more we can know ourselves, the better we are for public service. The more we can keep the higher motives in the dominant place in ourselves, the less likely we are to be driven from our course by being overblamed or overpraised. Public men are nearly always being overblamed or overpraised, and the more knowledge they have of themselves, the less likely they are to be unduly depressed by the one or to be unduly elated by the other.

There is a story which is useful for a man in public affairs to remember. It runs : that in olden times an oriental Sultan ordered his Grand Vizier to get engraved on his favourite ring a motto which would encourage him in adversity and keep him modest in prosperity. It had necessarily to be a short sentence, and yet it must serve this double purpose. The Grand Vizier was equal to the occasion. He advised the Sultan to have engraved on the ring the following sentence : " And this also shall pass away." This does not mean that our attitude is to be one of waiting to see it pass away : but it means that, being sure of our motives and our principles, we should hold them fast in success and should not be unduly depressed when we find things are not going as we wish. This latter aspect of the motto is specially to be commended in the present time, when things are certainly not going as we wish. It should encourage us to persist and to hold on to the course which we think right. At the present moment, when many things seem to be going wrong, although we may not be able to put them right all at once, yet if the country makes up its mind to stand by what it thinks is right, and if it hoists its standard, other peoples, although perhaps not immediately, may gradually rally round that standard.

To most people it is essential that they
should continually examine the motives from
which they act. There are a few exceptions,
men so happily constituted that they have little
or no need for this. Unconsciously, and without effort on their part, their motives remain
unselfish, sincere, and pure. I know no better
instance of that purity and unselfishness of
motive in a public capacity than the fourth
Earl Grey, in whose memory these lectures are
given. He was not without a just pleasure in
popularity and in good reputation. He was
not without a just sense and a proper pride in
the value of a distinguished public position or
office. But when he approached a public
question he became so possessed by enthusiasm
for the ideal, that no other motive except that
of promoting this ideal, without regard to the
cost to himself or the effect on his own personal
reputation, had any weight with him. It is
rare in a public man to have this quality in such
a remarkable degree. I had differences of
opinion with him on questions of the day, and
I dare say many of these lectures will contain
things with which he might not have agreed,
for you will never get men of active and able
minds who are all in agreement on all their
conclusions. Yet there can be no better
preparation for those who give these memorial
lectures than to reflect upon his life from the
point of view of the motives which inspired
him. He, at any rate, never lacked interest in
public affairs ; he was always enthusiastic and

unselfish, and his interest was ardent, sincere, and generous. One who knew him well said of him—and it was true—" He lit many fires in cold rooms." That is one high type of spirit which we need in our public men. That is the spirit which will make the lectures given here worthy memorials of him. That is the spirit in which I have tried to address you to-day— not so much to give instruction, as to consider where we are at the present time : how we can remedy some of the shortcomings of the present day, in what spirit we should try to solve our urgent problems. And my last word would be —in these difficult times, let us, as far as we possibly can, regard fairly and wisely these complicated questions whether at home or abroad, putting aside individual prejudices, earnestly striving to deal with them on their merits, adopting no popular conclusions which we feel to be unsound, but shrinking from none that we believe to be worthy and right, and doing our best to contribute to make a public opinion which shall be alert, interested, sound, and statesmanlike.

V WATERFOWL AT FALLODON

THE grounds at Fallodon are not large. There is no park. There is no lake. There are two ponds, the larger of them less than an acre, a flower garden of fair size, and I have enclosed round the ponds two or three acres of rough ground planted with trees and shrubs. That is the place in which the water-fowl have been kept. Three things are necessary if you wish to have a collection of water-fowl. One is a fence as nearly fox-proof as you can make it, for the ingenuity of the fox is apt to defeat the very best and cleverest of human contrivances. In the enclosure you must have quiet, because waterfowl spend, in the early spring when they are in pairs, some weeks looking about for nesting-places, cautiously and quietly by themselves, and if they find that they are watched, or should you come suddenly upon them, and they are disturbed, they will not select that nesting-place, and will not nest at all. So even in the case of one's self or the gardener, care must be taken not to walk at random in the nesting season on ground where birds are likely to nest, for fear of

destroying the chance of their nesting altogether. Quiet is, therefore, the second neces-
sity. The third thing necessary is that there
must be some one who gives daily attention to
the birds and takes an interest in them, and at
Fallodon that has been done all these years by
my gardener, Mr. Henderson, to whose interest
in the birds, and the great care he has taken
of them, is due the credit of such success as
has been attained in rearing the different
species.

Now I come, in the first place, to the list of
different kinds of waterfowl actually reared in
the collection at Fallodon. Of British surface-
feeding ducks, the mallard, wigeon, pintail,
shoveller, garganey, and teal—in all six kinds
of British surface-feeding ducks—have nested
and reared young ones. Of British diving
ducks, the tufted duck, red-headed or common
pochard, the red-crested and white-eyed
pochards—a total of ten kinds of British ducks.
Of foreign ducks, the Spotted-bill, Carolina or
North American wood duck, the Mandarin,
Chiloe wigeon, Chilian pintail, Bahama pintail,
Chilian teal, Rosy bill, Jalcated duck, Brazilian
teal, blue-winged teal, Japanese teal, and
versicolor teal—in all thirteen kinds of foreign
and ten of British ducks which have, at different times, been successfully reared.

I have distinguished, in giving the list,
between surface-feeding and diving ducks, and
this, of course, is a very usual distinction given
in books. But for the purpose of observation

of waterfowl, one most remarkable distinction is between those drakes which have an "eclipse" and those which have no eclipse. No doubt those amongst us who are interested in birds know what an "eclipse" is. The most striking instances of the eclipse are to be found in the most brilliant-plumaged drakes. Take, for instance, the Mandarin drake, or the Carolina drake, which are two of the most brilliant-plumaged waterfowl in existence—in fact, two of the most brilliant of all birds in existence. The females of these species are quite sober and dull-coloured birds, so that any one in the breeding season who knew nothing about the birds, seeing the duck and the drake together, would hardly believe they were related to each other, so different are they in appearance as far as colour is concerned. But somewhere between the middle of May and the early part of June these brilliant drakes lose all their brilliant colours and become quite dull like the females, so that anybody who did not know the birds well would have very great difficulty in seeing the difference between the ducks and the drakes. It is a most remarkable and striking change. In the case of most British ducks (there are one or two exceptions) all the drakes undergo the eclipse after the breeding season and become quite dull-coloured like the ducks. While this is the rule, generally speaking, amongst British ducks, it is not the rule with ducks all the world over. It is often not the rule in closely allied species.

Take the common wild duck or mallard. A brilliant and beautiful bird the drake is, in his best plumage ; he becomes in the summer quite shabby and has an eclipse. But take other birds of the mallard species : the spotted-billed duck in India, the Australian wild duck, the yellow-billed duck of South Africa, or the dusky duck of North America. They are all of the mallard species, so closely allied that they will mate and breed with other mallards ; yet the drakes of these four species have no " eclipse." The drakes are comparatively dull in colour, just like the ducks ; their general appearance is the same, and there is no great change in coloration during the year. Next I come to the instance of our common British wigeon. A most beautiful bird the drake is in his breeding plumage, but he becomes a brown bird in summer, and the females are dull-coloured. In the Chiloe wigeon, which is also a true wigeon, the drakes are gay-coloured birds and the females also are of gay colour. The result is that the drake has no change. He and the duck have practically the same appearance— he is a little brighter at one time than another, but both are gay in colour all through the year. The British pintail has just the same sort of eclipse and just as marked as the British wigeon ; while in the case of the Chilian pintail, so closely allied that to me the notes of the drakes of the two species are indistinguishable, the Chilian pintail drake is quite dull in colour like the duck, and remains so all the year round. So in the same way with the British teal and the Chilian teal ; there is the same resemblance in voice and there is the same difference in the habit of plumage as in the case of the two pintails.

Thus you have waterfowl divided, even in closely allied species—those which have an eclipse, and those which have no eclipse. And there is this curious difference which comes with the eclipse. Where the drake has an eclipse, he pays no attention to the female when the brood is hatched. For instance, the pintail is an early-breeding bird, and sometimes it brings its brood on to the water while the drake is still in his breeding plumage ; but whether he has come into the moult or eclipse or not, he never assists in the rearing of the brood at all. The Chilian pintail drake, on the contrary, which has no eclipse, goes with the duck and brood and takes just as much care of them as the cock partridge gives to a covey of partridges. I asked a friend, who had gone to South America to study wildfowl, if the same thing happened in the wild state, and he informed me that as far as he had observed it was so. When the drake has no eclipse he attends to and helps to bring up the brood. That is the curious difference of habit where drakes have no change of coloration during the year. What is the reason for it ? Why should this difference result in the drake in one case helping to bring up the young, and in the other case paying no attention to them ? These are

matters which require much more study and
which should be of much interest to those who
have the opportunity of following them up.
That is one point which is comparatively little
noticed, so far as I have seen, in books, and it
is of considerable importance to those interested in the habits of birds.

As to the actual breeding of the different
species, I can give you in the time at our
disposal only one or two instances of special
interest.

I would tell you of one incident in the breeding of the Carolina or North American wood
duck which I thought of considerable interest.
I had a good many of these birds at one time,
unpinioned, and therefore at perfect liberty to
choose a nesting-place. Their natural nesting-
place is apparently a hole in a tree. One of my
ducks selected a hole in an old elm-tree some
three hundred yards from the water. There
she nested every year and brought out her
young. The hole in the tree was a considerable
distance above the ground, and Mr. Henderson
(I was away at the time) was very interested to
know how the duck managed to get its young
brought down to the ground. One year he
noted the day she began to sit, and, as he knew
the period of incubation, on the morning the
duck was due to hatch the eggs he sat down
a little distance away opposite the elm-tree.
Presently he saw the duck come to the mouth
of the hole and fly down into the long grass
underneath, where she began calling. Then he

saw the little ducks come to the edge of the hole and fall, one at a time, except in one instance where two fell together. There were six of them, and he told me they fell like corks into the long grass. Afterward I had the height from the ground measured and the depth of the hole in the tree measured. The hole was two feet deep, two feet perpendicular from the nest to the mouth of the hole. The hole was twenty-one feet above the ground, so that the little ducks, newly hatched when the mother flew out of the hole, had first of all in the dark cavity of the tree to climb up two feet within the trunk, then come to the mouth of the hole and throw themselves down, and after having done that to go with their mother for three hundred yards through the long grass following her to the water. I think this is a striking incident. Think of the little ducks left in the nest. Newly hatched out, they had no feeding to strengthen them after leaving the egg. That they came out of the egg with such vitality and vigour that they could accomplish a climb of two feet perpendicular, and after falling twenty-one feet they could thereafter go three hundred yards through long grass, is a great tribute to the energy of Nature.

You will observe that the mother duck made no attempt to carry them down. I have read in books that the common wild duck occasionally nests at a considerable height from the ground. I have seen one nest about seven feet from the ground, and know that this is so ;

but when I see it stated that in such cases the mallard or common wild duck carries the young ducks down to the ground, I doubt it. I think if any duck is in the habit of carrying its young to the ground, the North American wood duck would do so, as its natural nesting-places are in holes in trees and not on the ground like our common wild duck. Since this North American wood duck made no attempt to carry its young down to the ground, I am doubtful if any waterfowl would make the attempt at all. I will not say it is impossible. I have seen the young cuckoo, naked, helpless, and unable to stand up in the nest, turn out of the nest a newly hatched young bird that I put in with it ; and having seen this, nothing to me in Nature is incredible. So while, judging from the wood duck, I am now of opinion that no waterfowl carries its young down from the nest, I will only maintain that opinion until some trustworthy observer assures me that he has seen it done.

The versicolor teal which were bred at Fallodon were, as far as I know, the only birds of this species that have been reared in this country. Of course, I cannot be sure. There may have been some instance I have not heard of. These bred once with me, and the sequel is curious. Eight were reared, so I had a little flock of ten beautiful versicolor teal. The sexes are so alike, as is the case with several other South American waterfowl, that young males and females are difficult to tell. Unfortunately, out of the eight that were reared, six turned out to be drakes and only two were ducks. However, that made three pairs of versicolor teal. One pair I exchanged with dealers for something else which was rare and which I wanted, then the old duck which had bred died, and the young pair left were in the following year killed by a fox which somehow got into the enclosure. I found myself left with five drakes. Then came the War. Of course, during the War I made no attempt to buy any birds or replace losses by purchase. Two drakes I sent to the Zoological Gardens. They had not the species at all and were glad to have them. I had then three drakes. I heard of one female of the species being in the collection at Kew. I thought it worth while to send one of my drakes to Kew to mate with the female which had no mate, so I did that. In the next air-raid a piece of our own shrapnel fell and killed the female at Kew. Soon after that food became impossible to get, and what remained of my versicolor drakes, in common with several other rare things, perished. That completed the episode. First of all, the interest and satisfaction of rearing birds never bred here before ; then the apparent security of having ten birds and the thought that I was sure to have representatives of this species in my collection to the end of my life ; and now not a single representative of the species left to me. That is the sort of thing that happens with the rare and much desired.

One other point I have selected to tell you about: the breeding of waterfowl. Of course, as you all know, wild ducks are monogamous and not polygamous like pheasants. They have one wife, and theirs is a very highly developed domestic life with great evidence of affection. Where the drake has no eclipse, the pair never separate during the year. Where the drake has an eclipse, he separates when in eclipse, and when he comes into plumage again, early in autumn—which most of the waterfowl do, though it is so long before the breeding season—the duck and drake come together again and spend the whole of the autumn and winter displaying every sign of affection in each other's company. The greatest instance I have seen of this is one that I will tell you. It was a red-crested pochard— a species very rare in Britain in a wild state. One drake that I reared was never pinioned, so that he could fly. I had him for over ten years, and during all that time he had never been away once. He mated with a duck, a bird of his own species, but which had been pinioned and could not fly. He spent years with her, and had every appearance of being happy and contented. One day, early in the year, his mate was injured by some vermin and practically ripped open on one side. She sat on the bank for two days perfectly helpless, and there he sat by her. She was so much injured that I had her caught and put out of her pain. There was another female pinioned, red-crested pochard unmated, and I thought, of course, that the now lonely drake would mate with her ; but he would pay no attention to her. He spent, if I recollect the time—it was some years ago—two or three weeks flying about with every sign of restlessness and distress from one pond to the other looking everywhere for his old mate. I had had him for some ten years, and he had never gone away, but now after two or three weeks he went. He flew away, and I never saw him again ; it was as if he had gone on an endless search of the world for the mate he had lost. That sort of thing is very interesting, for it shows the great natural affection which exists amongst birds of a highly developed and intelligent species. To me it is a clear proof of the fact that the relationship between the more highly developed birds is one of real domestic happiness, not confined to the breeding season and the reproduction of species only. I know that swans become attached to each other. You can see it is so. They do become permanently attached to each other, and have domestic happiness, which plays a large part in their lives, quite apart from the breeding season.

Perhaps you would like to know how long these sorts of birds will live. A great many of my birds are unpinioned and fly away, but in the case of a pinioned bird you can tell how long it lives. The longest-lived bird I had was a Chiloe wigeon drake. I bought him as a full-grown bird in October, 1888, and he died peacefully, and obviously of sheer old age, in October, 1908. I do not know how old he was when I bought him, and this is the longest life I have known of any of my waterfowl. For some years before he died he had shown very distinct signs of old age. He became very stiff, and infirm, and eventually was found sitting on the bank dead, obviously of old age. Geese, and larger birds probably, live much longer.

Since I have had these waterfowl of different kinds at Fallodon, it has been very interesting to see the varieties of wild ones which have come to my ponds. I remember when I was a boy my father showing me a place on one of the burns at home, and saying, " That is the place where I once shot a teal " ; and with that and one other exception, nothing but mallards, as far as I know, have ever been shot or seen on the actual property at home. It does not extend to the sea, and the sea ducks do not come to it ; but I myself once, after a great gale in the winter, shot an immature wigeon on a little pool. With these exceptions, nothing but the common wild duck used to be seen on the property at all. Now every year my ponds are visited frequently by the mallard, teal, wigeon, pintail, shoveller, pochard, and tufted duck. I treat the enclosure as a sanctuary. That shows how so many kinds considered rare by those who shoot, such as the shoveller, are often passing over, especially in the season of migration, and, if they hear birds of their own kind calling below, come down and settle. One very interesting point about wild things is how quickly you can get a perfectly wild bird tame. I remember one December afternoon finding a wild pintail drake on the pond. He rose, flew high into the air, and circled round ; but when he saw that the pinioned and tame birds did not follow him, after much flying at a great height he lit again on the pond. That evening when I was feeding the birds, he came and looked on, and within a week he would come out with the others to feed and pick up the grain I threw to him, and even when some of the grain fell on his back he was not alarmed.

So you see how tameness in their own kind gives confidence to the wildest birds ; but that tameness, that confidence, is associated with the place, and does not cause them to be less wild elsewhere than they were. I had one good instance of this in the case of a drake shoveller. A brilliant bird in full plumage, he came one year in February or March and stayed on my ponds. He was not always there, but he was often there, and he adopted all the habits of my tame shovellers. If he was sitting on the bank and I walked past, he would fly five or six yards into the water and sit quite unconcerned. If he was in the water, he did not offer to get on the wing at all. One day after lunch I walked round the pond and saw he was not there. I went for a bicycle ride, and coming back, about a mile from home, I saw on a

pool in a field, not on my property, a shoveller
drake in full plumage. I felt morally certain
it was the same drake which had come to my
ponds, because you do not commonly see a wild
shoveller in the district. The pool was about
one hundred yards from the road. I got into
the field and walked straight towards him. He
rose off the water, went high in the air, and
after circling about I saw him go straight for
my woods. I stepped the distance at which
he had risen, and, allowing for a few yards of
water, those I could not step, the distance was
something over ninety yards. I bicycled home
and went straight to the farther pond which he
usually frequented, and there he was on the
water, perfectly unconcerned and tame. That
is a very good instance of how quickly birds
find out when a place is a sanctuary. Really
it is worth while for anybody who has a little
bit of ground and a little patch of water to
have a few waterfowl and make it a sanctuary.

One more instance I will give of wild birds
tamed like this. I came home once in December after an absence of some months and found
that there was a pair of teal which had been in
the habit of coming to feed with my waterfowl
when no one was present. They were wild,
and when I showed myself at one pond they
flew to the other, and so forth. Gradually,
however, they began to come out and watch
the feeding of the others every evening. They
came out of the pond about twenty yards from
the spot where I was sitting. They came

cautiously round behind the trunk of a beech-tree, by a route that none of the other birds took, and drew nearer and nearer every evening until, after some four weeks, they came up a little behind me, a little to the right and about four yards from me, and I got them to pick up the grains I threw. That went on for some weeks. In March they went away, presumably to breed somewhere else. In August I was standing at the end of one pond when a drake teal in eclipse came flying and lit about ten yards from me. I thought, of course, that he had not seen me, and as soon as he saw me he would fly off. He took a look round, and when he saw me he never offered to fly away, but began to preen his feathers. I thought, "That is the little drake come back again. I shall know at feeding-time in the evening." At feeding-time he came out with the other birds and picked up the grain.

I could not be sure he was the same drake, but about the duck I can be sure. The drake stayed, came out of the eclipse, and got his full breeding plumage, but there was no sign of the duck until November. In November I was walking along the bank when a little duck teal flew off the bank and out on to the water a few yards. It remained there while I passed. I thought, "That must be the little duck come back for the winter. I shall see her at feeding-time in the evening." In the evening I sat at the foot of a big larch as usual, and the little duck teal came out of the pond, not

E

as the others came, but about twenty yards from the others, just in the same way as she had come in the previous winter. She came round the trunk of the beech by a route no other ducks took, and stood at the same angle and at the same distance as she had done before, and began picking up the grain I threw.

These little things—and I have had a great many instances of them—if you have an interest in waterfowl, these little things add extraordinarily to the interest of life. The sequel is a short one. She paired at once with the little drake, and I hoped they would stay through the winter. After three weeks they flew away. It is some years ago now, but for some time I cherished the hope that they would come back again.

My collection now is not what it was. I lost a great many birds during the War owing to bad food. I did not attempt to replace losses, and could not have done so in some cases had I tried. I have got a lot of birds still, mostly bred on the place, but I have not the same number of species that I had ; and now, partly because my sight is so much impaired, I find most interest in having as many as I can unpinioned, as tame as possible, and yet at perfect liberty. There is a sort of romance in having naturally shy birds, perfectly free and unpinioned, coming, as some of my wigeon and pintail do, to feed with perfect confidence out of my hand, while I know all the time that any day they may join the wild ones to go south in the winter or far north in the spring. They are naturally shy things, yet, when they are in this particular sanctuary, they are perfectly tame and have perfect confidence. If they should go away with the wild birds, they will be wild outside like others of their own species, and yet any morning I may go round the pond and find they are back quite tame again. There is interest, almost romance, in these happenings, and I know of no greater satisfaction for people interested in birds or animals than having wild things altogether free from control, naturally wild and shy, yet perfectly tame, so that they show you confidence and trust. You can observe their natural habits going on in your presence, which you could not do with the same species in the wild state, because their exceeding shyness and fear of man make it impossible freely to observe their habits till in some way or another you have convinced them that in one place at any rate man is not an enemy. Then you can have the great pleasure of watching close to you the colour of their plumage, their movements, their courting, their flight, and all the things that make them beautiful and interesting.

VI THE FLY-FISHERMAN

PALLODON PAPERS   130

VI THE FLY-FISHERMAN

A LL the papers in this book, with one
    exception, deal with matters of re-
creation or pleasure. A friend suggested
that something about fly-fishing should have
a place in it. To my plea that I had already
written a book about fly-fishing, he replied
that this made the omission of any special
reference to fly-fishing in the present volume
unseemly ; it was also more than a quarter
of a century since my book was written, and,
if I were to write about anything at all, it
was time that I wrote something more about
fly-fishing. He suggested " the character of
the fly-fisherman " as the aspect from which
the subject might be approached.

But has the fly-fisherman, as such, any
particular character ? Statesmen and politicians, divines and men of business and
affairs, artists, musicians and men of letters,
mechanics and artisans, people of both sexes,
of all temperaments and occupations, may
be met with amongst fly-fishermen. Even
the assertion that one who is devoted to
angling must needs be a good man is not

135

to be accepted without some question and searching consideration.

It seems preferable, therefore, to begin by saying what fly-fishing is, rather than by discussing the character of those who practise it.

Fly-fishing is an earthly paradise, and there is but one quality that is necessary to make us fit to enter into and enjoy it. We must be born with an intense desire to catch fish with a rod and line.

Fly-fishing is but one form of angling, and to enjoy it to the full a man must be born an angler. The passion may be latent, for years it may not discover itself owing to lack of opportunity, but if it is not revealed when opportunity comes, it is not there.

As a boy the real angler will fish for stickle-backs or eels, if he can get nothing better; the watching of a float will be to him a matter of undeviating attention and interest; the bobbing of the float when a fish bites will cause him excitement; the thrill that he will feel when a fish is hooked and is being played is indescribable; and the capture of a fish of relatively large size will produce exal-tation; the loss of such a fish after hooking it will afflict him with intolerable anguish. After a successful day, he will be in a glow of beatitude, but blank days will not dull the edge of keenness.

Perhaps only one who as a boy has known the excitement of small experiences can appreciate to the most exquisite degree the pleasure of the highest form of fly-fishing. The angler whose youth has found delight in catching small fish with bait on a short line has a standard of comparison, a measuring-pole of feeling wherewith to gauge the tremendous event of hooking a salmon with fly at the end of twenty yards or more of line. It is well to come through the smaller things to the enjoyment of those that are transcendent, and he who from his earliest youth has had the noblest forms of fly-fishing at his disposal is not necessarily to be deemed the happiest. But without insisting on fine gradations of pleasure, the main point is that for the highest zest and delight in fly-fishing a man must be an angler. He must have a keen desire to fish in the element of water and to capture with rod and line the fish that live there free and at large.

The man who has in him no sympathy for the humbler methods of angling, the salmon fisher, who despises trout fishing, the dry fly purist, who cares nothing for other methods of angling, in all these there is something lacking of the greatest pleasure that fly-fishing can give. Personally, when separated from my own opportunities of fly-fishing, I can never see an angler watching his float on the Thames without feeling a sense of envy, a desire to do what he is doing.

It is, however, rightly claimed for fly-fishing that it is the very crown and con-

E*

summation of the pleasure of angling : the reasons for this are many ; it is not possible to say what value is to be attached to each, but there is no doubt that all together in combination they lead to a decided preference for fly-fishing.

There is a sense of high art in inducing fish to take for food something which is composed of feathers and materials that have, taken separately in themselves, no resemblance to any edible thing whatever. This seems also to give the fish a more sporting chance than if a hook is concealed in a worm or a prawn or a minnow. Even the artificial minnow or the spoon is not so clever a contrivance as an artificial fly, made to resemble a real insect.

A further advantage is that, except with very large salmon flies, in using the artificial fly there is no sensation of weight at the end of the line, until a fish takes the fly. This enhances the contrast between feeling nothing of weight at the end of the line and the sudden connection with a ponderable and pulling fish. I have had too little experience of sea-fishing to have any right or desire to disparage it, but it has always seemed to me that the need for having a weight to sink the line was some diminution of the pleasure in hooking and playing a fish, and the same applies in degree to the use of heavy baits or lead in fresh water.

Salmon fishing in very early spring is one

of the most glorious forms of fly-fishing ; but one of the drawbacks to it is the enormous size of the flies and weight and length of the hook that the salmon prefer at that season of the year. The sensation to the angler is that of casting the body of a small bird at the end of the line all the time. There is perceptible increase in pleasure to the angler when in May the smaller and lighter flies become more attractive to the fish than the larger ones.

The lightness of a fly makes the use of a comparatively slender and lively rod, not only possible, but an advantage in casting, and the liveliness of the rod contributes greatly to the liveliness of the fish and to the pleasure in hooking and playing it. The numbness of a stiff rod is a drawback to trolling and heavier methods of fishing.

The continued effort and skill of casting is another advantage of fly-fishing ; the angler is always doing something ; and finally in trout fishing, generally, and in salmon fishing sometimes, there is the pleasure of seeing the rise, the motion of the fish as it takes the fly on or just under the surface of the water. Some of these advantages are shared by other forms of fishing. There may, for instance, be as much or more skill required when spinning for salmon or when fishing a North Country river for trout with worm on a bright day in June, when the water is low and clear, but there is no other

method except fly-fishing that combines all
the delights that are here attributed to it.

It is easy, while sympathizing with and
finding pleasure in all forms of angling, to
justify a preference for fly-fishing, but to
decide between the different sorts of fly-
fishing is more difficult. Of fly-fishing there
are three main divisions, each very distinct
from the others—salmon fishing, wet-fly-fishing
for brown trout or sea trout, and dry-fly-
fishing.

Let a sample of a day's dry-fly-fishing on
a chalk stream in the latter half of May be
taken first. The angler is by the river not
later than ten o'clock : the stream is lively
but quiet, and here and there the surface
is broken by the recurring swirl of a swaying
weed ; but no life disturbs it, except the
occasional dive of a dab-chick, the movements
of a watcher or water-vole. Not a bird
skims the surface of the water, not a fly is
to be seen on it, not a sign of living creature
under it. But the fresh light air is like a
caress, the warm sun shines interrupted only
by the occasional passage of small white
clouds, the water meadows are bright with
buttercups, and the woods and hedges that
are on their borders are white with haw-
thorn blossom or lit by the candelabra of
horse-chestnut flower. Birds of many sorts,
most notably blackbirds, are singing, and the
angler in his hour of waiting has such entertainment as seems more than imperfect man

can deserve or comprehend. Presently—it
may be seen or not till after an hour or more
—flies begin to appear on the surface of the
water, the rise of a trout is seen : in a short
time all is life and agitation. Trout are
rising everywhere, some audibly, some without sound ; flies are hatching out all over
the river, sitting or skipping in little flights
on the water or rising into the air ; a moving
network of birds, swifts, swallows, and martins, is on the river ; a rush of bird life and
the swish of the wings of the swifts is heard
as they pass and repass up and down the
stream ; and the angler, no longer inert, is
on his knees in the midst of it all, at convenient
distance from a rising trout, one arm in
constant action and the rod and line making
a busy sound in the air as he dries and casts
his fly. Now for two hours or more his life
is energy, expectation, anxiety, resource, and
effort. After two hours or so the rise begins
to slacken ; in time it becomes difficult to
find a rising fish, and the fish when found
is fastidious and hard to tempt ; and by
two or three or four o'clock, as the case may
be, the river has become as lifeless as when
the angler first stood by the bank in the morning. The water glides, fresh as ever ; the
weeds wave, but the rise of fly and fish is
over and swifts and swallows and martins
have withdrawn to the upper air, or to their
various abodes.

Consider another day about the middle of

June, a day of blue sky and blazing sun and
still air. The beginning and end of the rise
will not be so clearly defined as in May ;
there will not be the same exuberance of bird
life, though it will be even more abundant,
for many young birds are fledged ; but the
water meadows will be bright with even
more flowers than in May. The rise of fish
and fly will be more leisurely, but the angler
can spend more hours of the day on the river
with good hope of finding a rising trout ;
and there will be an evening rise that enables
him to fish for so long as he can see his fly
on the water. There may be less volume
of water going through the main hatches,
but the stream is still fresh and the river is
bank full, and the angler's basket may at
the end of the day be heavier even than on
the best day of May.

What is the wet-fly-angler doing now on
a Northern river, with its streams shrunk
to threads and trickles ?

I think of a stretch of the Itchen as I knew
it from 1885 to 1905, when sight was perfect
and I had comparative leisure and quiet.
There would be from twelve to eighteen full
days' fishing, spread over May, June, and
July, the average number of trout caught
each day (not counting those under one
pound in weight, which were returned to the
river) would be from two and a half brace
in an indifferent season to three and a half brace
in a good one ; and the average weight of

the fish ranged from one pound and a quarter in a poor year, up to a fraction less than one pound and three quarters in one year of supreme excellence. And every trout would have been caught on a fly not larger than oo and on gut never thicker than 3 X.

Each good day of dry-fly-fishing will have its own special memories : the big trout that was so hard to persuade ; that took one natural fly after another so confidently and ignored the artificial fly with such certain discrimination, but rose and was hooked at last and made off with a rush, as if it realized in an instant the mistake it had made after avoiding it for so long. There will be the catastrophes too ; . the big trout hooked and lost, others risen and not hooked and the failure with fish that could not be persuaded at all. A day's dry-fly-fishing ends with memories of large trout seen and noted, suffi-cient to provide further days of excellent sport.

Now let the wet-fly-angler have his turn. For him there is a wildness and variety un-known to the chalk-stream angler ; he needs skill to adapt himself to changing conditions ; he will fish upstream or across or downstream as circumstances may require or expediency prompt. Sometimes his river is full and brown, at other times low and clear ; he fishes rough water, rippling water, still water rippled by the wind, when it is calm and smooth. For this he needs great skill in

casting straight and far and fine ; and he
needs great knowledge born of experience
of the river in all conditions of weather and
water. He will no doubt make the most of
the hours when fly and trout are visibly
rising, but his sport will not be limited to
these hours ; he will fish the water knowing
where there is chance of a trout when no
trout are showing. For him there need be
no long minutes or hours of waiting and
watching for a trout to rise : he can be active
during all the time that he spends on the river,
never waiting about like a man out of a job.
If the dry-fly-angler pleads that his hours of
waiting give opportunity to enjoy the beauty of
nature, the wet-fly-angler may fairly retort :
" You may have felt that beauty when you
first stepped into the water meadow, but
from the moment you stood by the river your
eyes were on the water ; you were watching
for a rise, you were thinking of trout, your
whole attention was on the surface of the
water, though you were doing nothing and
not making a single cast. Your whole mind
was given to fishing, though in fact you were
not fishing : it was time wasted. For an
hour or more you did not see a rise, but you
dare not take eye or attention off the river,
lest a fish should rise without your seeing it.
With me, on the other hand, there is no hour
when the prospect is so hopeless as not to be
' worth a cast.' "

As for the character and surroundings of a

North Country river, its streams are rippling everywhere, while a chalk stream, except at intervals where hatches occur, is mostly silent. It is the wet-fly-angler, who knows best the "beauty born of murmuring sound." Of birds, which the chalk stream has not, there will be curlews, whose prolonged vibrating notes in spring are an expression of pure joy unsurpassed by any other bird sound ; the dipper, which with the feet of a land bird is equally at home on or under the water, in its ways the very embodiment of expert happiness ; and there is the pleasing company of oyster-catchers and sandpipers.

At the end of a good day in spring the trout in the wet-fly-angler's basket may average two, three, or four to the pound, but they will be numbered by the dozen, while those of the dry-fly-angler on a chalk stream are numbered by the brace. He will have had dozens of incidents and countless rises, and perhaps more than one adventure with large trout of one pound or even more in weight. The North Country trout in rivers of any size are more wild and strong in play than those of chalk streams ; the absence of weeds, and the open, and in places rapid, character of the water, give more scope and strength to the activity of a trout when hooked. It must, however, be stated on the side of the dry fly, that in certain conditions of weather and water its use may be more successful than that of the wet fly, even on a North Country river.

Of sea-trout fishing there is not space to
write here ; too often the best sea-trout fishing
is in the still water of lochs and must be
done from a boat. If the angler be by a
river, where fresh sea trout are running and
where he can cover them from the bank or
by wading, he is indeed fortunate ; there is
no other form of trout fishing that is the
equal of this in excitement and wild sport ;
but of such I have had too little experience.

The greatest of all sport in fly-fishing is
that for spring salmon in a big river. It is
in kind quite different from fly-fishing for
trout. It is only by courtesy that the arrangement of feathers, especially on the huge
hooks used in early spring, can be called a
fly ; and the motion of the fly in the water,
carried round by the stream at the end of
a long tight line, has no resemblance to that
of any known insect ; the fly works sunk
in the water, and in spring is generally taken
by the salmon without any break or sign
on the surface of the river. What the angler
expects is not a visible rise, but a sudden
tightening of the line by a strong and un-
deniable pull. The sensation of this pull,
especially if it comes after an hour or more
of casting and unfulfilled expectation, is one
of the great moments in the joy of life ; if
the salmon be well hooked, it is followed
by a period—it may be anything from five
minutes to half an hour—of intense anxiety

and strain, to be consummated, if all ends well, by a feeling of triumph and admiration, when the splendid beauty of a fresh-run salmon is contemplated on the bank.

The mention above of the time taken to play a salmon is based on normal conditions, in which one minute for every pound that the fish weighs is an estimate of the maximum time that should be required to bring a salmon to the net or to the gaff. If a fish be foul hooked, or if an exceptionally small rod and fine tackle are used, a longer time may be occupied, but in my experience it is very rarely that this estimate of time has been exceeded.

For perfect enjoyment of salmon fishing it is necessary that the angler should be on a river, to which the fish have reasonable opportunities of access : and he must be fishing pools where fresh-run salmon are wont to rest at that season of the year after entering and on their passage up the river. With these conditions present, the angler has no excuse for not fishing continuously and hopefully, unless the water be rapidly rising or abnormally high or low. He may, indeed, fish for hours without success, but there is always the fair chance that he may meet a run of fresh fish, and that unwonted success in the latter will more than compensate for failure in the early part of the day. The recollection of certain days on a big Highland river in May will serve as illustrations of variety of success in salmon fishing. The first sample was a day on which continuous casting (with a short interval for lunch) produced nothing till three o'clock in the afternoon. There had been not a pull nor a touch. Then at last came the pull and the hooking of a fish : after a few minutes' play, during which the fish jumped once and was seen to be about ten pounds in weight, the hook and the salmon parted company and the angler was still faced with the prospect of a blank day. But he had met a run of fresh fish at last and went home in the evening with three salmon weighing thirty, twenty, and fifteen pounds.

Another day began with the hooking of a heavy salmon in the first pool after only a few minutes' casting ; the fish played deep and steady, but like the first one on the previous day freed itself from the hook. From that beginning till late in the afternoon there was no pull or touch, but by the end of the day six salmon, including one of twenty-six pounds, had been landed. Blank days the angler must have sometimes, even when conditions are apparently favourable, but the experience and memory of such days as the two described above will keep him keen and alert, hopeful and expectant through hours of unrewarded casting.

Now and then comes the day when a combination of perfect conditions raises salmon fishing to a peak of enjoyment. A third day, also in May and on the same Highland river, shall be given as an instance.

Early in May the angler had been wrenched from the river by an untoward but compelling summons to London. Hateful as it was, the separation from the river was not so inopportune as it might have been. There were bitter storms and floods at the moment. Winter was vehemently opposing the advance of spring, and the angler left behind him a welter of storm and turbulent, unfishable water. In four or five days he returned, reaching the nearest station about ten o'clock in the morning after a night journey. At the pool at the top of the beat the gillie met him with rod and tackle ready for use as he had left it. Spring had come, the air was warm, the sun shone, the river was perfect in size and colour and likely to be so for some days, for it was high and falling very slowly. At this point the river comes round a corner between steep wooded banks, whence it flows away straight through more level and open country. After turning the corner the stream is broad and smooth, though strong to the tail of the pool. In this pool it was as certain as anything can be in salmon fishing that there would be fresh fish, and that in such conditions of water and weather following a spate, one or more of them would take a fly. For some moments the angler stood rod in hand looking at the broad brown stream, at the gleam of the sunlight on it,

and the small ripple of the surface made by
a very gentle motion of the mild air. It
is at such moments that hands tremble with
the excitement of anticipation and that the
angler enjoys the exquisite pleasure of it,
reluctant to put anticipation to the test of
reality by beginning to fish the pool. Here
he stood on the top of a golden hour and might
well pause for a moment to admire the prospect before him. Exceptionally perfect conditions of weather and water; the benign
contrast of genial spring with the winter of
a few days ago, his own keenness sharpened
by absence from the river and a few days
spent in town. Surely no one on earth
had before him a fairer promise of one happy
day !

And what came of it? Not a record;
nothing very great, but enough success to
make the promise good. Three salmon were
hooked and two were landed in the first pool ;
and the total for the day was eight salmon,
all of them fresh-run spring fish. With more
than one of them not only the whole forty
yards of the reel line, but the greater part
of the backing was also run out in the earlier
part of the contest; notably was it so in
playing the largest fish, one of twenty-five
pounds, which coming at the fly, perhaps
with mouth shut and intention of passing
over and drowning it without taking it,
hooked itself not inside the mouth, but outside in the chin. Besides the fish landed, four

were lost, two of them in the very last moments of play and when within two yards of the gaff. And the weather and the water continued to be perfect throughout the day.

It is ungracious and futile to compare the merits of the different forms of fly-fishing : salmon fishing, wet-fly and dry-fly-fishing for trout. Each, if it be good of its kind, has special charms and satisfaction of its own.

It has been said already that the pleasure of angling is not limited to fly-fishing, though this may be the most exquisite form of it. All anglers know what this pleasure is : it is too comprehensive and pervading to be described within the compass of words ; it is too subtle in some of its forms to be analysed ; too intimate to be explained : to those who are not anglers it cannot be conveyed, or made intelligible. The gift of the power to enjoy has various forms and diverse objects. There is no need for those who have one form of this gift to look askance at those who have another. But surely as life draws to a close no one can look back on days of recreation with more certain gratitude than he who has had the opportunity of fly-fishing and has been born with the gift of enjoying angling.

FIRST of all, let me say, that like many lovers of Wordsworth, I not only find "The Prelude" very interesting, but every time I read it the interest to be found in it grows wider and deeper and more intense, so that it ranks very high indeed in Wordsworth's work. This estimate of "The Prelude" is by no means universal. I once possessed—I am glad to say that I possess it no longer—a copy of an edition of Wordsworth in one volume, in which I was disappointed not to find "The Prelude." On turning to the Preface I found it stated that the volume contained all the poems of Wordsworth which were of real value, and that the only omissions were of poems such as "The Prelude," which were by general consent not up to the mark ; I have even found myself an object of pity to at least one literary friend for reading "The Excursion" or "The Prelude" at all. I once heard a distinguished man describe the speeches of another man also distinguished, whose speeches were full of learning, but more copious than inspiring, as being like a magnum of soda-water that had stood uncorked for a week. To some people, I fear, " The Prelude " and " Excursion " appear dreary and flat. As against their depreciation, I will read you an appreciation of " The Prelude " from a very unexpected quarter—the words are these : " When I came in after years to read ' The Prelude,' I recognized, as if it were my own history which was being told, the steps by which the love of the country boy for his hills and moors grew into poetical susceptibility for all imaginative presentations of beauty in every direction." I think I might safely say that no man or woman in this room, however great his literary knowledge, unless he already knows from whom that quotation comes, would guess the author of it. It comes from one who was apt to depreciate rather than appreciate many things about which others were enthusiastic. The words are those of Mark Pattison. You may set that unexpected appreciation of " The Prelude " against much depreciation of it ; Mark Pattison says here just what makes many of us feel Wordsworth a special poet, the sense that in him we find our own experiences reproduced. As we read him, we constantly find ourselves saying, " I know that I have felt that." And sometimes he reveals to us what we have not been previously conscious of, so that we say, " I have felt that without knowing it." Thus, to those of us who have the same sort of susceptibility that

Wordsworth had to all the aspects of natural
beauty, his poetry becomes something not to
be measured merely by poetic merit, but something which reproduces, interprets, and reveals
to us our own experiences, and is therefore not
like something outside appealing to our admiration, but like something which is akin to us,
part of ourselves, part of our lives. Therefore,
in speaking especially of " The Prelude," I am
not going to talk of its poetic merit or speak of
it as a poem, though it has passages which
seem to me of the highest poetical beauty.
I want to speak of it as what it really is, an
autobiography, a document of real authentic
human interest. It begins with a description
of Wordsworth's childhood and schooltimes,
and as you read on in " The Prelude," you
realize, or at least I realize, especially four
things about Wordsworth : his extraordinary
independence of spirit ; his resentment at any
restraint ; his deep and unflinching love of
liberty for himself and for the world ; and
finally, his firm conviction that it is not through
knowledge that we grow—unless that knowledge be accompanied by feeling—that great,
pure, exalted thoughts are due not to knowledge, but to right and elevated feeling. Those
four things I find coming out again and again
in " The Prelude." First take his childhood.
His childhood was really incredibly free. At
five years old, he was making " one long
bathing of a summer's day " in a small millrace
separated from the main stream. At ten years

old he was out half the night in the late autumn
or the early winter, alone on the hills, scudding
from snare to snare, which he had set for woodcocks, taking the woodcocks from his own
snares and sometimes taking those that were
not in his snares, but were caught in the snares
set by another boy. That act he knew was
wrong ; he tells us how the consciousness of
wrongdoing wrought on him ; he says :

> . . . and when the deed was done
> I heard among the solitary hills
> Low breathings coming after me, and sounds
> Of undistinguishable motion, steps
> Almost as silent as the turf they trod.

I will take one more passage parallel to this.
Again he does something that he feels to be
wrong. He finds a boat tied to a willow-tree
on a moonlit night. He looses the boat and
rows himself out on to the lake in it. It was,
he says, an act of stealth. As he rowed, taking
pride in his rowing, rising on his oars, he fixed
his eyes on a bare ridge above which was
nothing visible but the sky ; as he rowed
farther, gradually there opened up the view
of a high, dark peak behind the ridge, and as
he rowed on, the peak grew in height until it
seemed to be something great and immense
that was stalking after him. His conscience
smote him ; he took the boat back to the
willow-tree and he went home, but after that,
his conscience working in him, he was haunted
by the vision he had seen of the peak. In a

passage, too long to quote in full, he tells what
he felt, and he ends with these words :

> . . . for many days my brain
> Worked with a dim and undetermined sense
> Of unknown modes of being ; o'er my thoughts
> There hung a darkness, call it solitude
> Or blank desertion. No familiar shapes
> Remained, no pleasant images of trees,
> Of sea or sky, no colours of green fields ;
> But huge and mighty forms, that do not live
> Like living men, moved slowly through the mind
> By day, and were a trouble to my dreams.

I quote these passages to make this observation.
You observe that on both occasions he thought
in himself that the acts he had done were
wrong.   There is no trace that he felt any fear
of being found out, no trace that he dreaded
human censure or punishment by his guardians
or those who looked after him, or by any
human agency ; no trace of his caring for what
others might think of his conduct.   His own
conscience finds the reproof in what he thinks
he sees in the aspects of Nature ; and so you
will find throughout " The Prelude " an almost
abnormal indifference to human censure ; he
is never depressed by blame nor elated by
praise, but constantly worked upon by his
susceptibility to the outward aspects of Nature.
In that alone he found his education and
discipline. He goes on to describe various
things in childhood—all examples of a wonder-
fully free life—in words that bring home to us
the experience of our own boyhoods ; things

like his climbing cliffs for the raven's nest on a
precipice so steep that he seemed hardly to be
supported by foothold or handhold, but almost
to be suspended in air ;   and then he says :

With what strange utterance did the loud dry wind
Blow through my ear ! the sky seemed not a sky
Of earth—and with what motion moved the clouds !

Passages like this abound, and as you read on
and turn the pages you see " Schooltime,"
" Schooltime," " Schooltime," all through two
books at the top of every page ; and in the
text not a single mention of his once entering
a school, having any lessons or teaching or
discipline, any rewards or any punishment,
and he sums up at last by a passage—again too
long to quote—in which he says that he and
his companions loved sitting up late at night
till all other lights were out, scampering over
the country in the daytime, leading a life of
sheer pleasure so far as we can judge from
" The Prelude," innocent but uninterrupted
perpetual pleasure : and then there is this other
touch, that, though he sat up with his companions late at night, he would get up for his
own pleasure early in the morning, sometimes
going five miles around the lake before schooltime ; sometimes sitting alone in the wood in
the early morning, or on some promontory,
and then there came to him these feelings, even
as a boy, which we find so constant in his poetry
afterward ; the feeling as if bodily eyes were
utterly forgotten.   Finally comes this touching

tribute in blank verse to the place where the
days of his childhood were spent :

> Dear native Regions, wheresoe'er shall close
> My mortal course, there will I think on you ;
> Dying, will cast on you a backward look ;
> Even as this setting sun (albeit the Vale
> Is nowhere touched by one memorial gleam)
> Doth with the fond remains of his last power
> Still linger, and a farewell lustre sheds,
> On the dear mountain-tops where first he rose.

I quote that because Wordsworth did what I
have not known an instance of another poet
having done. He afterward wrote it in rhyme
and published it separately, and I will give it
to you from memory as it is in that form :

> Dear native Regions, I foretell,
> From what I feel at this farewell,
> That, wheresoe'er my steps may tend,
> And whensoe'er my course shall end,
> If in that hour a single tie
> Survive of local sympathy,
> My soul will cast the backward view,
> The longing look alone on you.

> Thus, while the sun sinks down to rest,
> Far in the regions of the West,
> Though to the vale no parting beam
> Be given, not one memorial gleam,
> A lingering light he fondly throws
> On the dear hills where first he rose.

You can read these two passages for yourselves,
the one in blank verse, and the other in rhyme,
and consider at leisure which you think the
better of the two.

When Wordsworth parts from school, when

F

his schooltime is over, he pays a tribute, not as
we mostly do to masters or to the spirit of the
school ; he says that he left school with his
heart pure, free from low desires, and that this
was due to the country in which he lived.

Now I pass from his schooltime to his time at
Cambridge. With that independent spirit of
his, he did not seem to find his entry into the
university formidable. We, most of us, who
have been to universities, in our first days, or
weeks, have found the beginning rather formidable. There is no trace that Wordsworth
found it so. But he did not get much good
out of the university ; he says he felt that he
" was not for that time or for that place."
One splendid tribute he pays to the statue
of Newton :

> Newton with his prism and silent face,
> The marble index of a mind for ever
> Voyaging through strange seas of Thought alone.

A tribute he pays also to Milton, but con-
nected with the name of Milton there is an
incident in " The Prelude " of a lighter kind.
He drank wine in Milton's rooms with some
friends, and he poured out libations to that
famous memory until his head grew dizzy with
the fumes of wine ; he is careful to tell us that
this never happened before or since. About
this incident I must relate the story of an
admirer of Wordsworth arguing with some one
who did not admire Wordsworth. The former
found himself confronted with the argument

that Wordsworth was a prig without any natural weaknesses. I suppose if he had known the phrase, the critic would have said, "Without one redeeming vice." The admirer of Wordsworth in defence said, "Well, at any rate, he got drunk once." "Yes," said the other, "I know he says so, but I am afraid his standard of intoxication was lamentably low." I put that on record as a lighter touch. Wordsworth proceeds to say in justice to Cambridge that, if he got little good from it, the fault was his own, and not that of any one else, and, having thus satisfied his conscience by blaming himself, he then goes on to say how unedifying he found the place. He said of the Dons, "They served to set our minds on edge and did no more." You can compare that with Gibbon's more flippant statement about his tutor at Oxford, "He remembered he had a salary to receive ; he only forgot he had a duty to perform." You cannot read "The Prelude" without feeling that the strictures on the university had, at any rate, some truth in them in those days, but let me say at once that nothing of that kind is true to-day. If the universities of the eighteenth century were dead, it is true of them to-day that they are living parts of the nation, that those who are most concerned in their teaching are most careful to keep in touch with the political, economic, and social thought of the day, and Oxford and Cambridge, with other universities, are to-day living parts of the nation's life.

Wordsworth closes his description of Cambridge with an extraordinarily powerful passage describing what he felt not only about those in authority, but about the undergraduates as well :

> Idleness halting with his weary clog,
> And poor misguided Shame, and witless Fear,
> And simple Pleasure foraging for Death ;
> Honour misplaced, and Dignity astray ;
> Feuds, factions, flatteries, enmity, and guile,
> Murmuring submission, and bald government,
> (The idol weak as the idolater),
> And Decency and Custom starving Truth,
> And blind Authority beating with his staff
> The child that might have led him ; Emptiness
> Followed as of good omen, and meek Worth
> Left to herself unheard of and unknown.

And so he parts from Cambridge.

I have now spent much time and I have not got beyond his university life. I must pass over the part about his summer vacation, although it has that very important and interesting passage in it where, in the presence of a splendid sunrise, alone after a night of revelry, he feels that he is ever afterward to be a dedicated spirit, and having said that and described that experience, he says :

> . . . on I walked
> in thankful blessedness, which yet survives.

I want you to notice those last three words : " which yet survives."

" The Prelude " was written, not in extreme youth, but when he was in the thirties, in the prime of his poetic gifts and power, and that emotion of his early youth still survived. Most of us have these moments of great emotion under peculiarly favourable conditions of outward circumstance. We all recognize, or at least most of us must recognize, having felt amongst particularly grand or beautiful aspects of Nature what Wordsworth felt on the occasion of that memorable sunrise ; but with most of us the emotions are like a breeze upon a lake, making its ripple at the time and then leaving the lake as it was before. With most of us, it is not so much that we are incapable of these great moments of great emotions as that they are, as far as we are concerned, rather like writing in water. With Wordsworth it was not so. They lasted. The substance of which he was made was something so tenacious that, when these great moments of emotion came, they wrote indelibly upon his personality ; their effect was cumulative ; they built him up and made him the great poet that he was, and those words " which yet survives " would apply, no doubt, to many of those great moments in his life. It seems to me that one of the special characteristics of Wordsworth in his youth was this combination of extreme susceptibility with great tenacity. This was a quality in Wordsworth which I think accounts for very much of the poetic excellence of what he wrote and for the power which his poetry has.

I come now to the next book, which is

headed " Books," and I would observe two
points about it, which are : (1) that he states
absolutely and without qualification that for
the young there should be complete liberty in
reading ; there should be no restraint upon
their choice of books. I know that this must
be a very controversial subject ; personally, I
side with Wordsworth. He takes the homely
simile of a hen with her chickens, and he
applies that to the supervision over the reading
of the young. He says :

> Behold the parent hen amid her brood ;
> Yet doth she little more
> Than move with them in tenderness and love.

I would observe, however, on this simile that,
although it is absolutely true to the life of what
some birds do, or appear to do as regards their
young, when the young are able to feed themselves, the mother bird does lead the young
where the best food is to be found, and I think
a fair summary of Wordsworth's view of reading for young people is that they should be put
in the way of the best literature, and should
then be left to choose for themselves what they
like best. (2) The other point is that knowledge got from reading will not do us good
unless it produces real feeling ; that emotion
must accompany knowledge. He pays a great
tribute to what he owed to books, but he says
he got from them knowledge with continually
increasing joy, " knowledge not purchased with
the lack of power " ; and he has a long passage,

and an exceedingly good one, in which he expresses his scorn of the prig who reads merely in order to acquire knowledge without thereby growing in feeling and sensitiveness. Here are a few lines of it :

> . . . he sifts, he weighs ;
> All things are put to question ; he must live
> Knowing that he grows wiser every day
> Or else not live at all, and seeing too
> Each little drop of wisdom as it falls
> Into the dimpling cistern of his heart :
> For this unnatural growth the trainer blame,
> Pity the tree.—Poor human vanity,
> Wert thou extinguished, little would be left
> Which he could truly love ; . . .

And then comes a burst of enthusiasm and contrast at the end :

> Oh ! give us once again the wishing-cap
> Of Fortunatus, and the invisible coat
> Of Jack the Giant-Killer, Robin Hood,
> And Sabra in the forest with St. George !
> The child whose love is here, at least, doth reap
> One precious gain, that he forgets himself.

Well, that has wisdom in it for all of us who are in search either of knowledge or pleasure. We get neither in their highest form unless we seek them in such a way, with such enthusiasm, with such feeling that we forget ourselves. It is true we find ourselves thereby, but we find ourselves by forgetting ourselves. That inability to forget one's self stands more almost than anything else in the way of the use people make of knowledge or of gifts, and

stands often in their way even when they are
trying to find pleasure. I think one of the
saddest things, as you reflect on the history of
the world, is the mischief which has been done,
the opportunities which have been missed, by
men with great powers in great place being
unable to forget themselves. It is a natural
failing. The greater a man's powers, the more
difficult it is for him to forget himself, and it is
only when you come to the very great men of
the world, whose greatness of soul and strength
of moral purpose were greater even than their
great powers, that you find the men, who in
public affairs have had great opportunities
and risen to the full height of them and done
all they might for the world. The ending of
that passage :

> . . . doth reap
> One precious gain, that he forgets himself,

is one of far-reaching wisdom and interest.

Now I must pass on to another part of " The
Prelude " altogether, for I must, before I
finish, say something about Wordsworth's
experience in the French Revolution. It had
a remarkable effect upon him as a young man,
and no study of Wordsworth's life, no appreciation of his work can be thoroughly intelligent
without reading carefully that record, which we
find given directly in " The Prelude " and
indirectly in " The Excursion," of his experiences in France. He first went to France on
his way to the Alps. At that time the States-

General had been summoned, and, though the
Monarchy had not been abolished, there was
a belief throughout France that the day of
Liberty had come, and that the old bad times
were past, and the description Wordsworth
gives of the rapture manifest in the whole
country is very powerful and very touching.
He says :

> France standing on the top of golden hours,
> And human nature seeming born again.
> Lightly equipped, and but a few brief looks
> Cast on the white cliffs of our native shore
> From the receding vessel's deck, we chanced
> To land at Calais on the very eve
> Of that great federal day ; and there we saw,
> In a mean city, and among a few,
> How bright a face is worn when joy of one
> Is joy for tens of millions. Southward thence
> We held our way, direct through hamlets, towns,
> Gaudy with reliques of that festival,
> Flowers left to wither on triumphal arcs,
> And window-garlands. On the public roads,
> And, once, three days successively, through paths
> By which our toilsome journey was abridged,
> Among sequestered villages we walked
> And found benevolence and blessedness
> Spread like a fragrance everywhere, when spring
> Hath left no corner of the land untouched ; . . .

" War shall cease ; did ye not hear that con-
quest is abjured ? " the peasants say to him,
and we realize what a fair face the dawn of the
French Revolution had. I recalled this description when I was at the Foreign Office at
the time of the Young Turk Revolution. We
had reports then of people belonging to different

races, between whom there had been bitter
enmity, now greeting each other as brothers,
and in a still shorter time than in the French
Revolution, things went back, not to the same
despotism of Abdul Hamid, but to one worse,
if possible, than that before. What happened
in the beginning of the Russian Revolution
I do not know so well, because I was not in
office at the time. As we read the description
in Wordsworth of the beginning of the French
Revolution, we realize all that he felt, and all
that the young literary spirits of the day felt,
about it. They felt that man was naturally
a being intended for good, and of great dignity ;
that he had been kept back by the barriers of
an old system ; that the Revolution had swept
away these old barriers, and that man for the
first time in civilized history was going to be
free, to advance toward what was his natural
heritage, to what he deserved, and to what was
his right. You must read carefully to realize
the natural enthusiasm that Wordsworth and
others like him felt. Then came the beginning
of bloodshed and violence. Wordsworth did
not ignore this, and its incidents he called

Ephemeral monsters, to be seen but once !
Things that could only show themselves and die ;

but when he found England going to war with
France, while he thought that in France was
the fairest hope, indeed the whole hope, and
the promise of human liberty and happiness,
he felt it bitterly. He described his feelings

in a stern passage where he says that if he went to church and heard prayers for the victories of the British forces, he felt as if he were sitting there " like an uninvited guest " whom no one owned, and instead of praying for the success of the British forces, he " fed on the day of vengeance yet to come." Such was his love of liberty, such was his feeling when he saw England in arms against France, and when he thought that Liberty was on the side of France ; but when France became the aggressor, when he became convinced later on that the cause of Liberty was with his own country and the cause of the aggressor and despotism was with France, then he produced that strong, patriotic war poetry which during the last war my friend, Sir Arthur Acland, collected into a volume, and which was no doubt read by many people and gave them, through the distress of war, something of that strength of spirit with which Wordsworth went through the distress of the Napoleonic Wars. When France became an aggressor, and exhibited the horrors of the Terror, nothing could surpass the bitter disappointment that Wordsworth felt. His disappointment was great in proportion as his hopes had been high ; he gives a powerful description of the distress of mind and the despair through which he went. At one time he says he " yielded up all moral questions in despair " ; yet he never doubted what the real cause of the French Revolution was : nothing could shake his moral judgment about this.

When other people were pointing to all these
horrors and saying :

> Behold the harvest that we reap
> From popular government and equality,

Wordsworth, in spite of his distress, says :

> I clearly saw that neither these nor aught
> Of wild belief engrafted on their names
> By false philosophy had caused the woe,
> But a terrific reservoir of guilt
> And ignorance filled up from age to age,
> That could no longer hold its loathsome charge,
> But burst and spread in deluge through the land.

And when he saw Europe beginning to attack
the French Revolution, and attempting to
put it down, and re-establish the Monarchy,
though he was not blind to the violence and
the bloodshed of those who were then in power
in France, he says :

> In France, the men, who for their desperate ends,
> Had plucked up mercy by the roots, were glad
> Of this new enemy. Tyrants, strong before
> In wicked pleas, were strong as demons now.

Thus he pronounced a wise political judgment
upon the unwisdom of interfering with the
Revolution from outside. In the whole of
Wordsworth's account of the Revolution, there
is nothing with more insight than this wise
political judgment ; there is deep political
wisdom in it for all similar occurrences, and
if these words,

> . . . the men, who for their desperate ends,
> Had plucked up mercy by the roots, were glad
> Of this new enemy . . .

whenever a great Revolution takes place in a foreign country, were hung on the walls of rooms where Cabinets meet, we might have been saved, and the French Government with us, from the mistake of spending millions in trying to crush the Bolshevist Revolution in Russia. The Bolshevists were the men who "plucked up mercy by the roots" in Russia. Wordsworth would not have been more sparing in his condemnation of them than he was in his condemnation of the Jacobins, but we might have remembered from the great events of French history that in such times interference from outside has, as a consequence, results directly the opposite to what is intended and hoped. As it was in the French Revolution, so it has been in the Russian Revolution. Finally, when Wordsworth "yielded up all moral questions in despair"—and this is my last point, to illustrate one more great characteristic of Wordsworth—he does not sit down under that despair. Whatever depression he goes through, he never ends the poem until he has found the thought which sets him on his feet, upright, above depression. You find it in poem after poem. However great the depression, and it was at times as great as ever poet had, he never rests until he has found the point of view and the thought in which he can be strong again ; where, instead of being a pessimist, he can be hopeful, sanguine, certain as regards the future. Thus, in his depression in the French Revolution, he finds hope at last,

and finds it through the help of his sister
Dorothy Wordsworth, who leads him back to
the influence of Nature. I will give this
quotation, coming after he had " yielded up
moral questions in despair " :

She whispered still that brightness would return ;
She, in the midst of all, preserved me still
A poet, made me seek beneath that name,
And that alone, my office upon earth ;
And, lastly, as hereafter will be shown,
If willing audience fail not, Nature's self,
By all varieties of human love
Assisted, led me back through opening day
To those sweet counsels between head and heart
Whence grew that genuine knowledge, fraught with
     peace,
Which, through the later sinkings of this cause,
Hath still upheld me, and upholds me now.

And there he gets strength again with the help
of his sister, by his suceptibility to the influences of Nature. It is in that susceptibility
to the influences of Nature that the greatest
strength of his poetry lies. I have read somewhere that when Wordsworth writes :

> One impulse from a vernal wood,
> May teach you more of man,
> Of moral evil and of good,
> Than all the sages can,

we must not take him seriously, for the impulse
of the vernal wood can teach us nothing. But
this in truth is the very root of Wordsworth's
own growth and education. Without the
impulse from the vernal wood he would not

have written his poetry, without that and many other impulses akin to it. This does not mean that the vernal wood consciously taught him ; it means that looking on the vernal wood he was raised to heights of sensitive feeling without which he would not have had the great thoughts that inspired his poetry. It is this susceptibility to outward Nature, that Wordsworth had in a supreme degree, which draws all those who have it, even in less degree, to his poetry and makes them satisfied. Reverence, pure delight, tenderness, love, these things he felt because the aspects of Nature, their beauty, and their grandeur, had inspired these feelings in him. To those of us who love Wordsworth, those moods, those exalted moods, which he had under the influence of natural beauty, though we may not have them so intensely or so often as he had them, are well known, as something which we recognize in our own experience. Simple lines of Wordsworth, for instance : "and that still spirit shed from evening air"; "motions of delight that haunt the sides of the green hills." " The silence that is in the starry sky ; the sleep that is among the lonely hills " ; even such a simple line as " Here are we in a bright and breathing world," stir us to a mood like his own. To those who are familiar with Wordsworth, a single line may be sufficient to bring us under that sweet influence, that powerful influence of the beauty of outward Nature which gives us some of the best moods in our life. One of the greatest

gifts that man can have is to be able to get
such moods as Wordsworth calls :

That serene and blessed mood,
In which the affections gently lead us on,
Until the breath of this corporeal frame
And even the motion of our human blood
Almost suspended, we are laid asleep
In body, and become a living soul :
While with an eye made quiet by the power
Of harmony, and the deep power of joy,
We see into the life of things.